To Myl

Keep Dreaming
Big!

Bratm

偉
大
的
奔
跑

The
Great
Run

CONQUERING THE
SLEEPING DRAGON WITHIN:
LIFE'S LESSONS ON THE RUN

BRAAM MALHERBE

Foreword by Professor Tim Noakes

SUNBIRD
PUBLISHERS

To Benjamin, who
showed me the meaning
of unconditional love.

May your journey be
wonderful, wild and
free. May your spirit
soar and love be always
in your heart.

Contents

TITLE PAGE Moonrise over the Wall.
PREVIOUS PAGES On the mud Wall during our recce trip.
THIS SPREAD The fort at Jiayuguan with Qilian mountains in the background.

Foreword

By Professor Tim Noakes

BETWEEN 24 AUGUST AND 15 DECEMBER 2006, Braam Malherbe and his close friend David Grier became the first humans on record to run the full extent of the Great Wall of China. They measured its distance at 3,515 kilometres – although they covered a distance of 4,218 kilometres due to having to leave the wall to find their support crew for replenishments on many occasions. After the pair had completed their run, the Chinese government declared the Wall off-limits to any future runs. Thus their achievement is unique and perhaps forever. What are we to make of those who are driven by ambitions that most of us cannot even begin to comprehend? In this book Braam offers some personal answers.

At 12, inspired by the stories of Tom Sawyer and Huckleberry Finn from another continent, he undertook his first solo 'boy's adventure' spending some nights on the slopes of Devil's Peak before returning home to his relieved parents, who must have thought that they had lost their errant son forever. On the mountain, alone and close to nature, he had discovered his childlike passion. Five years later, as a 17-year-old sometime runner who had yet to run more than 10 kilometres in a single run, he covered 532 kilometres in 11 days from Plettenberg Bay to Cape Town. His goal was to raise money for a study to determine the environmental impact of a proposed solid jetty in the environmentally sensitive Langebaan lagoon on the Cape West Coast.

When told the run was impossible, he reasoned that the fact that something had not been done did not mean that it could not be completed successfully. As a result of his triumphant teenage intervention, a more appropriate jetty was constructed in the Langebaan lagoon without negative environmental consequences. Then, at age 31, he ran 620 kilometres from the Tsitsikamma National Park to the Table Mountain National Park to raise awareness and collect money for the purchase of equipment to be used against poaching in the national game parks.

Thus the twin themes of Braam's life are clear – a passionate desire to educate others of the need to protect the environment, and the capacity to perform physical feats that others have deemed impossible. Which brings us to the focus of this book, his run with David along the Great Wall of China.

Professor Tim Noakes (left) giving David and me advice while doing eccentric training on the Grucox machine at the Sports Science Institute of South Africa.

At the start of this century there were two places on Earth that had yet to be reached by humans – the South Pole, first reached by the Norwegian team of Roald Amundsen in 1911, and the summit of Mount Everest, reached by Tenzing Norgay and Edmund Hillary in 1953, six years before Braam was born. Thereafter all that remained was the moon, which was first visited in 1969, when Braam was 11. To have been young in the 1960s was special, for it was a time of great optimism and self-belief. Humans really did believe that, given the willpower, we could achieve the impossible. To achieve a landing on the moon with the use of less computing power than is present in the most humble modern laptop computer was a quite remarkable feat. But, short of walking around the moon, there were not many remaining physical adventures on our planetary system that had not already been completed. Except the Great Wall of China.

When Braam first spoke to me about his desire to run the length of the Great Wall, it is true I told him it was improbable, perhaps impossible. I had assumed it would not be possible to run 42 kilometres a day, six days a week, on an uneven surface for more than 17 weeks without suffering a significant injury. And this did not even begin to consider the risks imposed by the environment, the risk of significant illness, the isolation, the altitude, the heat and the cold. It is also true I spoke about the failed British expedition to the South Pole in 1911, on which Captain Robert Scott and his polar team had man-hauled their provisions 10 hours a day for 159 days across the barren ice, covering just 16 kilometres a day. To achieve this they had expended more than 900,000 kcal of energy. But they had not survived. At a cost of 100 kcal a kilometre, Braam and David would have to expend more than half the total energy used by Scott's party and nearly three times as much energy as that used by cyclists in the modern Tour de France. So I had good reason to tell Braam that to complete the run across the Great Wall of China in the manner he proposed was as close to an impossible undertaking as I could imagine.

This book explains why I was proved to be wrong. The physical challenge in an event like this is not where the outcome is decided. For the body is merely a slave to the mind. And if the mind can be convinced of the value of the task, there is little that is impossible. But the full scope of the brain's seemingly limitless actions is constrained by the character of its owner.

Braam is driven by a character that is powered by honesty, passion and tenacity. His honesty is based on a complete understanding and acceptance of himself. Without that honesty, the run would have fallen apart at the first significant challenge. His honesty explains Braam's transparency that shines through his every pore. His passion is for the environment and for those less fortunate. So the ultimate beneficiaries of his and David's self-less run were the children born with facial deformities, now correctable within a few hours by appropriate surgical intervention – the Cipla Miles for Smiles campaign. His tenacity is such that he will not consider stopping until the task he has set himself is done.

This book is an inspirational testament of what can be achieved when good character and the pre-pared mind confront the ultimate challenge. Perhaps the greater question is why such human achievements are so astonishingly rare.

For the reality is that the world and the environment need many, many more Braam Malherbes and David Griers.

Professor Tim Noakes, OMS
Discovery Health Professor of Exercise and Sports Science
at the University of Cape Town and the Sports Science
Institute of South Africa

The crest of the final hill before heading down to the Bo Sea.

Acknowledgements

THE EXPEDITION ALONG THE GREAT WALL of China would not have been possible without the support of many people.

Our sponsors: Cipla, Devco Africa, Adidas, the Sports Science Institute of South Africa, the Health Junction, Trendmark Signs, EAS, Garmin, Santam, Medac, Klas Varki, Cape Union Mart and Vodacom.

The people who believed in me, motivated me, assisted me and stood by me: Dr Willem van der Merwe, Dr Wayne Derman, Dr Andrew Bosch, Prof Tim Noakes, Morné du Plessis, Shelly Meltzer, Amanda and Sammy Jo Nortje, Ulrich Meggersee, Georgie Ravenscroft, Clinton Gähwiler, Jason Chin, Mandi Wyngaard, Cathy Chambers, Sean Surmon, Belinda Guillot, Leanne Raymond, Shelly and Hugh Knyvet-Knevitt, Nicole Chamberlin and Geoff Smith.

My team in China: William Lindesay, Lunga, Piou, Lilly, Lee, Changa, Little Chang, Michael Rainier and Hans Seer. And my friend, David Grier.

I also want to acknowledge my Mom, late Dad, brothers and sister, as well as my late Uncle Dan and Aunt Velia for being such an important and special part of my journey.

My publisher, Sunbird: in particular publisher Ceri Prenter, editor David Bristow and designer Pete Bosman – and Les Martens for putting us together. Debbie Simons for her last-minute help and Hedda Inderthal for her guidance, vision, love and support.

To all of the above and to everyone who helped make this journey possible, I extend my most sincere thanks.

Lessons from the Great Wall of China

THE GREAT WALL IS REPRESENTED as a sleeping dragon in Chinese folklore. When I stood on a lonely plain of the Gobi desert and issued my challenge, like a latter-day knight, or Don Quixote perhaps, it awoke and raised itself to face the affront. In all its years, centuries and millennia of existence, it had not yet been beaten.

In 2005 Cape Town chef David Grier had hatched a foolhardy scheme, to run the main intact length of the Great Wall of China (3,515 kilometres) in one go. If completed as planned it would be a world first. I knew it would be forbiddingly tough – near impossible. But what I didn't know was how my journey along that monument to human endeavour, and indeed through that haunting land itself, would change my life and influence my outlook on just about everything.

During those long months in China I was to discover that the Great Wall is a metaphor for life: like the Chinese, we all build walls around us to protect us from perceived fears and dangers. All too often these walls, initially constructed to safeguard, become prisons to our imagination and prevent us from reaching our fullest potential. We bury ourselves beneath painstakingly contrived masks and personas and so forget our true selves. Conquering the Great Wall of China forced me, step by tortuous step, to deconstruct my own walls. It also made me question many of my deep-seated and ingrained beliefs.

More than once I stood at that razor's edge between giving up and carrying on, between death and life. One of the things my journey along

Feeling exhausted and seriously cold towards the end of a tough day. I had to dig deep and constantly remind myself of the big dream.

the Wall confirmed was my belief that we hold the key to our future in our hands. The outcome is determined by the decisions we make throughout our lives.

It is ironic that many people awaken to the gift of life only after staring death in the face, after something dramatic or painful reveals the fragile and fleeting nature of their existence. Only in our most dire situations, whether in war, or alone in some seemingly Godforsaken place, can we grasp the value of the gift we've been given on this Earth and that we should use it to the best of our ability, and maybe even aim beyond that.

Running the Great Wall end to end – we eventually clocked 4,218 kilometres – gave me the rare opportunity, in those many weeks and months of silence, to reflect, learn and grow. It was a huge and intense physical challenge, but it was just as much of a mental challenge.

A Wild Child is Born

I often like to think I represent the average outdoor, nature-loving guy, but with experience I have also come to realise (slow as it has been to penetrate my obstinate and determined head) that I have made choices that set me on a different and singular course. From my earliest memories I had crazy

Looking for a route across the badly eroded Loess plateau. The land here has been so exploited it is unlikely that it will ever recover.

ideas. All kids do, but I seemed to act on mine more than others, to always push myself just that little bit further, testing myself and the patience of those around me.

Like other children with access to a bit of veld, I spent hours and hours watching bugs, birds and animals and seemed to perceive some unifying truths about the universe. In my case those feelings never left me and the need to be at one with nature only grew stronger as I searched further. I guess I was, and have always been, a wild child.

At the age of 12 I didn't just think about running away from home, go to the end of the road and then remember it was time for dinner and head back. I took off for a week on my first foray 'to the mountain' to gain wisdom. Later, when I was at high school, I embarked on an ultra-marathon run with a friend during the September break – 532 kilometres in all – running after a conservation dream. I had not done anything remotely like it before and it made me believe that anything was possible if my dreams were big enough. It was the first time I realised that the difference between success and failure was all about mental attitude.

Even at that stage, if I'd had the self-knowledge that came later, I might have realised that I had chosen – always chose whenever I got half a chance – the path of most resistance and maximum adventure. Not just adventure for the sake of adrenaline that seems to be in fashion, but a path that would lead me to greater personal wisdom, as well as a greater understanding of the issues facing us as the custodians of this fragile planet.

As I grew up and moved away from my family base, I realised I would never be able to come to terms with who I was until I managed to unravel the complicated relationships within my family. Running the Great Wall gave me both the time – endless days, weeks and months of putting one foot in front of the other in a haze of pain and monotony – and insight that maybe only an extreme pursuit like this can give a person.

Tortured events, failures, losses, seemed to unfold in my mind and resolve themselves one by one. I came back from China a different person … or at least a changed one from the bundle of ego and energy that ran off into the Gobi desert, in the blistering heat of an alien land, that day back in July 2006.

Keeping Promises

The Great Wall turned my life around, and yet again reminded me of what's *really* important in life: family, loved ones, and safeguarding our natural environment, as these are the things that ultimately sustain us.

Subsequently, my task is to make good on all the promises I made to myself about my relationships with the people I care about, and using whatever time and resources I can muster to help preserve the beauty of this unique planet. Not just for our sake, but for all life and the many generations still to to come after us.

This amazing adventure on the Great Wall of China led me through a magic door in my life that otherwise I would have never even known was there, to a place of greater consciousness. I have gained so much understanding of myself, my place in the world, and the legacy I want to leave behind.

So this is my story. I hope you enjoy the journey.

Braam Malherbe
Appleton Camp, Signal Hill
Cape Town
February 2010

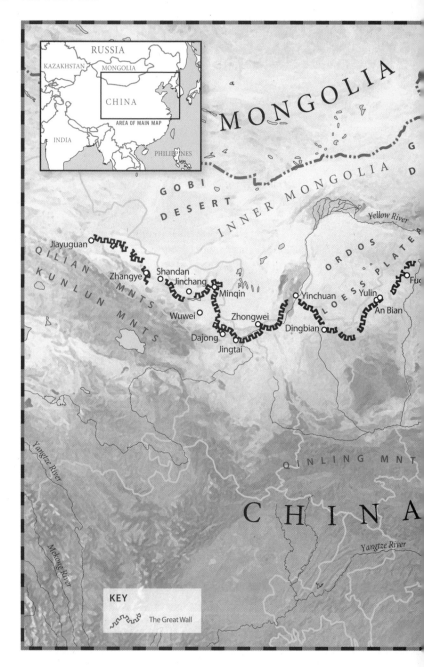

PART I

THE RECCE
Meeting the
Sleeping Dragon

偵察 — 相遇沉睡的巨龍

1

Alone

HOT, SHIMMERING, ORANGE MIRAGES of desert landscape stretching out as far as I can see. Sometimes flat, often undulating hills of powder sand or ancient broken stone – the vastness of the Gobi desert is daunting.

I am standing at 39° 48′ 073″ N and 98° 12′ 85″ E. This is the extreme western terminus of the Great Wall of China. The first lonely mud watchtower stands on the precipitous edge of a cliff with the Great White River some 200 metres below. The only flowing river in a vast, parched and lifeless land; its flood cycles have carved a natural barrier that in times past prevented the hostile, invading Mongol hordes entering China from the north-west. The Great Wall is a man-made double front, lying like a giant sleeping dragon across the country's northern frontier. It stretches from Jiayuguan in the west to Shanhaiguan at the Bo Hai (Sea) in the east. The vigilant, guarding dragon lies quietly for an estimated 3,500 kilometres.

Date: 24 August 2006; time: 13h00. Although it is autumn in the Gobi, the temperature is still in the high 30s. Standing here with my long-time friend David Grier, we are both silent. With every breath the hot air scorches the inside of my nostrils; my throat is dry and the sun feels like it is burning holes into the back of my cap. Each of us is holding a silk flag. Me, the flag of my country, South Africa, its bright rainbow colours shining in the sunlight, bringing a vibrancy to the dry and barren landscape. David holds high the red flag of China with its gold stars in acknowledgement of what we are about to begin.

We are going to attempt what many had said was impossible: to journey the entire length of the Great Wall on foot, in a single attempt, running (or crawling if it came to that) an average of 42 kilometres – or a full marathon – a day, six days a week, allowing for one rest day each week for recovery. We would be crossing some of the harshest terrain on the planet: from vast deserts with temperatures in the high 30s, through eroded lunar-like landscapes to high, snow-covered mountains where temperatures would be in the minus 20s. We wanted to travel the line of the Wall as closely as possible in order to measure its actual length by Garmin GPS. If completed as planned it would be a world first.

For a project of this kind to be really successful, careful planning is critical. First comes the dream, then the plan, only then the action. David's dream of running the Great Wall of China had been born some three years earlier, although I instinctively felt the idea of something like it had been in me since I was a young boy. It's a dream I think is in many children: the dream that we are superheroes, adventurers and explorers, and that we are invincible. That the Earth is a giant playground, rich with treasures waiting to be discovered. Now, standing in the barren desert, a frighteningly alien land, I vividly recall how it all started....

David phoned and said he wanted to meet to discuss what he called 'a crazy idea'. Over the course of a long afternoon involving many cups of coffee we exchanged ideas. I told him about my unerring determination to show children that nothing is impossible if you just believe in yourself enough.

He in turn spoke of his fascination with the Great Wall since he was a boy. He mentioned a documentary he had watched on the late Sir Edmund Hillary, the first man to summit Mount Everest. It was a tribute to the man some 50 years later. Hillary recounted how, on revisiting base camp, he had been disgusted at the litter of discarded oxygen cylinders, the crowds, human faeces and rubbish. The great mountaineer spoke out in anger and pain for what he saw happening to the sacred mountain.

'This was my Everest,' he said. 'Go and find your own Everest.'

David and I discussed the so-called impossible challenges of the world, those natural obstacles that tease the psyches of adventurous spirits – the obstacles that invite us to test ourselves and our abilities against the majesty of the natural world. As the first step towards 'finding our own Everest' we counted off the great challenges: the poles had been reached, by various methods; Everest had been climbed; the Earth had been circumnavigated this way and that; the Atlantic paddled. And here was one of the great challenges of the world standing before us, as yet unclaimed.

We began investigating the feasibility of running the full length of the Great Wall of China from start to finish in one go. The Great Wall, in the minds of many, and certainly in mine, is the greatest engineering feat in human history. The mighty pyramids of Giza pale into insignificance by comparison. It is said the bricks of the Great Wall could circle the Earth at the equator in a wall a metre thick and 1.5 metres high.

The idea thrilled me. I felt that familiar tension in my gut; the excitement I feel when something great or special challenges me, when I climb a difficult rock face, or am about to hurl myself out of an aeroplane.... The drone of the aircraft engines is the only thing I hear and my pumping heart is the only thing I feel. Then I leap into space. As I fall, I remember my Ouma (or Granny) when I asked her, at the age of about six, when I would be able to fly. I remember her saying, *'My engel, mens kannie vlieg nie, ons het nie vlerke'* (my angel, humans can't fly, we don't have wings).

But there I am, falling at 220 kilometres an hour from 25,000 feet. I push my right arm outwards while keeping my left arm tucked in tight, arcing across the sky without wings.

Going beyond the limits of ordinary human abilities and imagination seems to have been my calling from the womb. We are all awed by great achievements. They excite us and take our breath away when we realise the ability to confront them is inside each of us: all we have to do is to say 'yes' and take the first step. It's right there; it's real and tangible. We all have the potential for greatness and the desire to excel is in our blood. We just don't all seem to have the will.

As far as I've always been concerned, it doesn't make sense to play at being small. We deny ourselves our destiny in doing so. It is when we step outside our comfort zone that the excitement wells up and we know we are on a road to greater things. Well, that's the way I feel it, for sure.

I felt the Great Wall could be my great challenge, to prove to myself and others that nothing is impossible, even after many knowledgeable people had said it couldn't be done. It had not yet been done. But in order to make it happen I had to dream it vividly and often: I needed to add colour, material form and substance to my dream. I knew also that many people and situations would try to prevent me from achieving my dream. These would include the obstructive beliefs of people who subscribe to negativity as part of a habitual lifestyle, as well as the normal day-to-day pressures of feeding body and soul and also of caring for others close to me. I knew that in order to reach my goal, I would need to make the dream a part of me, a part of my everyday life, to let it burn like an inextinguishable flame and to not allow one breath of doubt to enter my sacred place.

2

William

SO WHY HAD THE GREAT WALL NEVER BEEN TRAVERSED from one end to the other in a single attempt? Why had no-one run it as we intended to do? Many had tried, none had succeeded.

'But why?' I kept asking myself, trying to untangle a bird's nest of circular reasoning and doubt.

I found my answer not while exploring the Wall and the extreme terrain it crosses, but in researching the climate. You cannot run in the Gobi desert in summer when temperatures reach into the high 40s and the area is scoured by murderous dust storms. Almost yearly, people there get trapped in these storms and perish. They die of suffocation as the fine wind-driven powder mixes with their saliva and clogs their throats and noses.

What I didn't know was just how much of a taste of this I was going to get about a year later.

Equally, you cannot run in the high mountains when the Siberian winter approaches, when the temperatures dive into the minus 30s before the mountains bend down to the Bo Sea. Nothing survives for very long in those extremes of climate and temperature.

I knew what that meant: a time frame of some four months and being exceptionally fit. The old cliché of survival of the fittest would be tested to a fine degree. To cover the Wall's 3,500 kilometres in the time available, we would need to move at a rate of around a full marathon a day, for close on four months. I also knew that the Wall did not exactly present ideal running terrain. We would have to run wherever we could, and walk, crawl, clamber and climb where we couldn't. But we would need to cover the necessary distance every day as planned if we wanted to survive and succeed in our quest. I also knew we would be moving from days with up to 11 hours of daylight in the Gobi desert, to very short and icy winter days in the high mountains with only six hours of daylight. Any injury could mean not only failure, but also possible death in the remote reaches of the Wall, where no-one would be able to come to our rescue.

Still, the more I learned and the longer I dreamed, the more tangible it all became. I could almost taste it. It was frightening and maddeningly exciting at the same time. The idea began to haunt me in my dreams and my waking hours. The bug had bitten hard, but first we had to plan well – logistically, mentally, physically and, for me, spiritually. David had sourced a book written by a man who had journeyed the Great Wall some 20 years earlier. William Lindesay had travelled the length of the Wall in various stages over a period of a year or so. He had been deported, but had returned. He had suffered dysentery, but returned. He seemed tenacious and, from what I read, I liked his attitude. William had met and married a local woman, and settled in Beijing with her and their two children. He had founded the International Friends of the Great Wall and is director of the organisation. He clearly had a deep knowledge, respect and passion for the Wall and its long history.

'Perfect,' I said. 'He's our man!'

Now it was just a matter of getting him to reply to our many e-mails. Where was the ever-elusive William? I had read his book, found out so much about him and the Wall, but William seemed to be a ghost. For agonising weeks we just couldn't track him down.

Then one day, some three frustrating months and countless e-mails later, a reply arrived. The ghost had finally materialised!

'I get inundated with people wanting to visit the Wall. Most have no idea what they're in for, but you chaps are certainly persistent. You appear to be serious about this. Perhaps you need to come to China and see for yourselves what you're getting into?' He was testing our commitment.

It took another three months of e-mails and phone calls before things gelled and William agreed to meet with us in Beijing to 'discuss things'. We planned a trip to meet him, to recce the Wall at various points and put the whole thing into perspective.

David and I arrived in Beijing in March 2005. It was summer and it was hot and muggy. My first view of the Wall was on a massive mural as I exited customs at Beijing airport. It looked picturesque, surreal, like something out of a *Lord of the Rings* movie. It certainly felt inviting, which maybe was a good sign, but I knew that perceptions could be very misleading.

We had booked into the Great Wall Sheraton, a lavish luxury hotel in central Beijing. The Great Wall was everywhere – murals, bank notes, on my visa, even the make of a vehicle. But, just like William, the real Wall remained frustratingly elusive.

William's driver collected us early the next morning for a three-hour drive, heading north of Beijing where we were due to meet William at his farmhouse in the mountains. Never in my life had I seen such an integration of First and Third World living. Silver-mirrored skyscrapers stood out like gigantic crystals in the grey hazy smog. The freeways were congested with traffic, from modern sedans to lumbering trucks and then, in a lane dedicated to slower traffic, bicycles and tricycles, some motorised, others being pedalled or pushed, with their huge, disproportionate loads of vegetables, scrap metal or massive oil drums balancing precariously. And everyone hooted! It was standard practice to hoot. Indicators were an occasional added extra. Traffic circles were a nightmare – just get in first and keep moving. I was baffled. There seemed to be no logical system in place. Even pedestrians would step off the sidewalk and head into the sea of heaving, hooting hysteria. But somehow it worked. People swerved and hooted. No-one swore and no-one crashed.

All around Beijing lines of trees were growing. This is meant to bring more oxygen to the gasping city and relieve pollution. The bases of most trees were painted white for about a metre above the ground. It's a poison to keep the ants and other invading insects at bay. I wondered who the real invaders were, because the masses of people reminded me of nothing so much as giant insects. In the shadows among the trees were many conical sand heaps, each surrounded by a ring of stones. Occasionally, at the top of the cone was a fist-sized rock or two. I discovered they were graves. Later, I was to see many more of them in the desert.

The grey haze stayed with us some 100 kilometres further as we wound our way into the hilly land beyond the city. I peered through the sad, oppressive metal-grey gloom and saw a fine line tracing the far ridges of the high mountains. Was this my first glimpse of the real Great Wall? I couldn't be sure.

Snaking along narrow dirt roads, weaving between slow, yoked oxen heaving their cumbersome burdens of wood, we entered what appeared to be an ancient village. The only real signs of modernity were the electric wires linking the homes like scattered spaghetti.

When the car could go no further we gathered our packs and wound our way up a narrow footpath, passing an old woman grinding maize on a large, obviously ancient mill stone. She smiled politely as I passed, acknowledging my presence in silence.

At the top of a gentle slope, an open gate made of plaited sticks was the humble entrance to a farmhouse. And there stood the elusive William!

He was a tall man, around six foot two inches (two metres), with a mop of silver-grey hair, excited, shining eyes and a broad smile. He loped across the courtyard and shook my hand in a warm welcome: the beginning of a special relationship. Over dinner that evening, which consisted of the tastiest fresh trout cooked by William's cook Lilly (who was to be our expedition cook more than a year later), I listened to William as he shared his knowledge of the Wall. He was so passionate that I grew more excited by the minute. I wanted to see it now, touch it, smell it ... I wanted to take a bite of my dream.

An early night was necessary as we would be up at 04h00 for a quick breakfast of farm eggs and toast before commencing our hike to finally make acquaintance with – what mountaineers call rubbing noses with – the ever-distant Wall. The door to my room was painted bright red. The ornate lock in the latch had a beautifully embroidered tassel hanging from it. The door was half open and it was dark inside. I paused for a moment to ponder the significance of this: red representing danger, yet the lock and the door being open, inviting anyone who was curious and maybe foolish enough to enter. What a metaphor for this mad journey we were planning. I took a deep breath and stepped inside, just as I committed to our plan of running the wall. Now that we were here, having made the long and expensive trip from Africa, there was no going back.

I lay on my thin mattress on the raised communal cement bed. These beds are common throughout rural China, probably originally made from clay. They are hollow underneath with a small opening on the outside of the building. This allows for a fire to be made under the bed, which warms the cement slab in the freezing winter. I lay in the dark contemplating my future and the changes that might occur. Looking back now, I realise I had no idea how these first steps towards my dream were going to alter the course of my life. I felt a little like a child first finding that it could walk, taking uncertain tottering steps, yet feeling great excitement at the new and wonderful discovery. I drifted into a restless sleep.

I got up at 03h30 and went outside to take a pee. The northern stars were still dazzlingly bright and so different from my familiar constellations back home. Everything I sensed was new and I was filled with a deep, craving fascination. Even the trees and grasses were different. Everything was a discovery. After putting on my running gear I hastily packed some basics into my day pack: camera, binoculars, compass, note pad and pen, some health bars and water.

In the greyness of dawn the three of us walked towards the mountains, our silence mirroring that of the land around us. Following William through green forest with dappled light as the predawn turned to dawn and dawn to day, sunlight at times flashing in my face, we wound what seemed like forever upwards. Rounding a bend, with the sun fully up, suddenly, there, through a small clearing, less than a kilometre away – the Wall, majestic and ancient.

I had goose bumps and couldn't speak as I walked over broken bricks piled around the base and onto the Great Wall of China for the first time. It seemed so long ago that I had dreamed of this moment. I leaned with my face and naked chest embracing the wall. I removed my running shoes and walked barefoot for the rest of the day. I wanted to really feel the connection. Seeking out the pain underfoot so I could get a feel for what things might be like day after day, week after week, month after month when we returned for real. That's when and why William gave me the name of the White Bushman.

To say the defensive barrier is impressive would be an understatement. The granite foundation blocks are, on average, about a metre long by half a metre wide and slightly less than that in height, weighing nearly a ton each. These blocks were hand chiselled in the valleys some 2,000 metres below and hauled up near-vertical cliffs using pulley systems. The smaller bricks that make up the higher sections of the Wall, the ramparts, walkways and watchtowers, were baked in village ovens as construction advanced across the country. They were carried manually on wooden L-shaped rucksack-type frames, up the steep slopes to the construction site. During the Ming dynasty (1368–1644) something like 90 per cent of China's population was contracted – mostly by force – to work on the construction.

It is estimated that one builder died for every metre of wall built.

The cement, too, was made in the valleys below. Glutinous rice porridge was boiled in huge pots, powdered limestone added and, incredibly, this paste still holds much of the Wall together today. The stark stone and brick watchtowers with their magnificent barrel vaults were cool and haunting. Standing in the silence, I imagined the long-gone soldiers talking, joking and laughing over a meal. I imagined a Mongol invasion – fires and columns of smoke, signalling from tower to tower across the rugged mountain tops that battle was at hand. I could hear the clatter of armour; see the oil being heated in cauldrons ready to be poured on the enemy below; arrows being carefully aimed through the specially designed window slots in the parapets; and, on occasion, the explosion from a hand-hurled bomb in the valley below (earlier in the morning I had seen shrapnel fragments of these bombs on the path leading to the Wall), and all the while the soldiers shouting in the heat of battle.

There were endless stories locked into the silent, cool mass of the Wall, so many memories of stories of so long ago, now only to be imagined. What an incredible feat of human imagination and engineering. A real tribute to visionary and tenacious (if tyrannical) leaders who held a nation together with a common goal, from dynasty to dynasty over the many centuries. This kind of steely, far-sighted resolve can be seen in much of what outsiders view as the contradictions of this amazing, if mysterious, country.

The shadows lengthened and it was time to leave the Wall and descend into the darkening valley. I had covered about 25 kilometres of extreme gradients and my feet were really hurting.

'Will I feel this pain each day when I come back?' I asked myself. I hoped not but feared I would. As I walked in silence, reflecting on the day, I felt a sudden tightening in my gut. There was sadness here. I stopped suddenly. David asked me what was wrong.

'Listen,' I said, 'just listen.'

'What?' he replied, 'I can't hear anything.'

'Exactly,' I answered.

In this beautiful forest, high in the mountains, at a time of day when the birds should be calling to each other, there was not a note. No bird, or even insect, signalled its presence. I realised I'd not seen any animal tracks on the paths either. Apart from the trees and us, there was no sign of life at all. I gasped at the sterility, while contemplating the obvious: pretty much anything that could be caught and eaten had been. The natural order was out of balance here. Again, I was harshly reminded that there are just too many people to be provided for, and how much more intensely you can see this in China – the world's most populous nation.

I arrived back at the farmhouse with mixed feelings. There was excitement and exhilaration at my first encounter with the Wall. My dream was tangible at last, but there was also a harsh realisation of how severe the damage already was that people had inflicted on nature in so many places. I was tired and emotional as we shared our feelings over another superb 'Lilly' dinner in the dark valley. As I drifted into sleep on my hard bed, images of the lonely, cold Wall high on the ridges above me swirled in my mind, morphing into fantastic shapes and evil dragons that were set to come back and haunt me.

3

An Egg and the Earth

I WOKE IN THE DARK FROM PAIN. My feet were throbbing. I had been dreaming about the first long run I had done as a kid. I remembered how my feet had hurt so badly I swore I would never subject my body to pain like that ever again. I had a slightly convulsive feeling akin to nausea and felt afraid. Pain is a real leveller and, with the vividness of my dream, I wondered what I was getting myself into – again!

On the long, winding drive back to Beijing, I reminisced on why I had done that long run all those years ago. I remembered clearly that it had been a strong conviction to protect innocent animals and nature from human carelessness that had carried me through those painful kilometres and set me apart from other young boys of that age.

In physical form I'm your average middle-aged man, if a bit lighter and somewhat fitter than most men of my age and place. I come from an outwardly pretty average family who lived in a middle-class suburban environment. Acquaintances would probably say I'm more hyperactive than most, but I still see myself as a pretty normal guy. So why is it that I seem to be drawn to do things that your average person would dismiss as crazy?

I am the eldest of five siblings and was taught to be responsible from a young age. As a child, I often had to look after my younger brothers and sister, having to make up for the inadequacies of my parents, who tended to be too caught up in their own problems to really worry or care. Among other things, I believe it was this forced independence that caused me to question the actions of adults and other authorities and measure things on my own moral compass. I felt extremely protective of my younger siblings, which later translated into a strong passion to protect all things dear to my heart.

When I was 16 years old I was fortunate and privileged enough to have been sponsored to attend a Wilderness Leadership School in the Umfolozi game reserve (now part of the Hluhluwe Imfolozi Park) in Zululand, a particularly wild and lovely, lush tract of subtropical bushveld in South Africa. This experience had a deep and profound impact on me.

Sitting in the shade of an acacia tree on a hot day deep in the Umfolozi wilderness area, which is totally devoid of any human structure, our ranger and guide Colin Johnson handed each of us boys our lunch ration. It consisted of a sandwich and a hard-boiled egg.

Colin asked us not to break the egg, but just to hold it and look at it.

He held up an egg and asked us the question: 'If this egg is our Earth, what part of it would be the air that surrounds us?'

We all said 'the shell'.

He was silent for a moment, before cracking the egg on his head. He carefully and slowly peeled the shell away, exposing the thin, delicate membrane that lay beneath. Lifting a piece of the opaque skin away from the egg, he held it to the light.

'This is how fragile our planet is,' he said slowly. 'This thin membrane is the only thing protecting us from whatever lies beyond. This is our thin layer of atmosphere and we must protect it at all costs.' He was silent for at least a minute and so were we. There was such stillness in that wilderness, with the occasional, mournful call of a green-spotted wood dove. Even then, so long ago, I felt frightened at the vulnerability of our planet. The memory is still vivid to me.

After the silence Colin asked a simple question, a question that changed my life: 'You are privileged to be here,' he said calmly, 'on this course and on this Earth. What are you going to do to make a positive difference to our Earth, when you get back to school?'

He did not say 'when you finish school', or 'when you retire one day' but '*when you get back to school*.' He was not giving me the escape that so many people use: 'one day, when I have time'. He meant *now*!

I did feel privileged. I had grown up with all the amenities and comforts a person could possibly ask for, and taken the resources our fragile ecosystems provided me with every day just as much for granted as everyone else around me. I realised then that if we didn't take care of and protect the Earth, we would be doomed.

And so it was, through the challenge issued to me by Colin in 1974, that I consciously began my journey towards discovering my true calling. He had challenged me to be a champion and protector of nature, which deeply resonated with the love and awe I had felt all my life for all things natural and pristine, as well as my protective personality.

I was also a junior member of the Wildlife and Environment Society of

South Africa at the time. Through the society I was made aware of the large concrete jetty being built into the beautiful Langebaan lagoon at Saldanha Bay on the south-west coast of South Africa. This was to be the terminal point of the Sishen-Saldanha railway line that would bring iron ore from the Sishen open-cast mine in the arid region of the Northern Cape, to be loaded onto vessels for export to the East.

The loading jetty, if built as a solid structure out into the lagoon as proposed by the task-focussed engineers, would significantly alter the flow of currents in the lagoon, with potentially catastrophic results for the flora and fauna endemic to the lagoon – a major wildlife and conservation area, especially for breeding colonies of sea birds. Some of them, like the Cape gannet, bank cormorant and black oystercatcher were already on the endangered list.

I was shocked at the blatant disregard for the voiceless plight of nature, with only the Wildlife Society seeming to care. I chose to do something to prevent the potential destruction: it was less than a year since Colin had issued his challenge to me and the other boys in that Zululand wilderness.

I approached a school friend, James Siddle, and outlined my plan: I wanted to run an impressively long distance to raise awareness – and money – so that an environmental impact assessment (EIA) could be carried out and a possible disaster prevented. EIAs were a new thing then and viewed by engineers and planners as something of a tree-hugging nuisance in those days. In fact, it has been proved that a properly conducted EIA will not only reduce negative impacts and increase the positive ones of any large development, but they save the developer money too by taking into account many variables that a strictly engineering point of view never would.

James was his usual keen self: 'We could run from my folks' holiday home in Plettenberg Bay back to Cape Town,' he offered enthusiastically.

'Cool,' I replied, 'how far is it?'

'Ah, around 500 kays,' was his casual reply.

Now, for pretty much any seasoned adult long-distance athlete, 500 kilometres is a serious distance to cover. For me, who was an average member of the school cross-country team and had never run more than 10 kilometres, it was almost unimaginable. Perhaps it was beautiful ignorance, coupled with a youthful passion to make a positive difference that made me believe it was possible. Sharing my excitement with my peers and teachers, I was told by most of them it would be impossible. As a degree of disillusionment set in I was faced with what might well have been the defining decision of my life: was I going to believe in myself, or in others? I figured that just because it had not been done did not mean it was not doable.

In 1975, at the age of 17, I ran with my good friend James from Plettenberg Bay to Cape Town – a distance of 532 kilometres – in 11 days. I remember that I experienced intense pain and that we had to stop for a day because my feet were so swollen. I also remember the cortisone injections into my ankles and the long road stretching out forever in front of me. I recall that each day my big goal became increasingly short, very short.

'Just get over that next hill,' I would tell myself, then you can reward yourself with a stop.

But I seldom did.

Running up that last hill to Rhodes Memorial, on the slopes of Devil's Peak, I felt like a giant and that I could achieve anything I put my mind to.

I had broken some kind of physical barrier and James and I achieved our goal. Together with our schoolmates we raised R18,000 and the EIA was done. As a result, the jetty in Langebaan lagoon was built on concrete columns that allowed a relatively unobstructed current to flow through the sensitive area and no species have been lost to extinction.

I believe it was that achievement, after Colin Johnson had showed me how fragile our Earth was and challenged me to do something to protect her, that has set me apart and made me understand fully that we are all unique and destined for great things. I realised that one individual can make a significant difference and, as long as you are driven by a cause that is real and sincerely touches your heart, you can do anything.

Hillary did it. Captain Scott nearly did. People like Jane Goodall, who is passionate about chimpanzees, have made an indelible difference in protecting our primate cousins in east Africa. Wangari Maathai saw the devastation of Kenya's forests and rallied women around her, explaining the importance of trees to subsistence farmers and others in her native country. Together, they planted over a million trees and for this she was awarded a Nobel Peace Prize. These people are linked by a common thread: they are driven by passion and see obstacles as things to be overcome en route to their goal.

As we drove in silence towards Beijing, my mind rolled back in time, connecting the various dots of my life. I remembered things I had not dwelt on for many years, seeds my Dad had sown so long ago. It felt like a dream as my conscious thoughts drifted out the car window across that alien Chinese landscape.

4

Family Matters

MY DAD HAD FREQUENTLY TOLD ME THAT, as the eldest of five children, I needed to be an example to my sister and brothers.

'Lead by example,' he would so often say. 'Be strong and walk your talk.'

I believe, as a result of that, and even though I felt lonely at times, from a young age I saw myself as a leader. After that first long run in 1975, my dad reiterated what he had said to me so many times before that.

He said it quietly and slowly: 'You see, I told you, if you believe in yourself you can do anything.'

My father was an Afrikaner, descended from the early French Huguenot colonists, and the eldest of four children. My mother was an English-speaking South African, descended from somewhat newer arrivals. Although my father was a publisher who specialised in Afrikaans books, we spoke only English at home. He was a wonderfully creative man and was very lateral in his approach to life, even though his upbringing had been rigid and conservative. He had been a Spitfire pilot in the Second World War. However, his path to being a fighter pilot was by no means a straight one. While training, he crashed his Tiger Moth bi-plane and broke his back. Lying paralysed in his hospital bed, he could hear the doctors discussing how he would never walk again. He could also hear the Spitfires taking off each day at the training base.

It had been his dream to be a pilot. He decided to hold on to his dream and ignore the negative prognosis of the doctors. He vowed he would fly. Every day as he lay in recovery, the sound of the powerful Rolls Royce Merlin engines reinforced his resolve. And so, day by day, week after week, month in and month out, he healed. And then he flew again.

He flew sorties from Cairo over the Mediterranean, up the spine of Italy, pursuing the enemy through Yugoslavia to Zagreb where he was shot down. Enemy fire raked his engine and he was severely burned by fire-hot engine coolant escaping from the nose. After undergoing many months of operations and suffering immense pain, he carried his scars into the post-war world.

Because of the high morphine doses administered to my dad in the war, he was prone to chemical addiction. He could not touch alcohol. Even a mild dose of sherry taken inadvertently in a Christmas trifle could send him into a dark downhill spiral, his only chance of recovery to detox in hospital – there were no plush rehab centres in those days. These bouts happened every few years.

For the rest, he was a keen businessman with a passion for books and for life in general. He was also a talented artist with an eye for detail, something I am lucky to have inherited.

But while I was growing up at home he was no hero to me. I got to hear some of his stories only towards the end of his life. In fact, in my early teens I thought of him as a weak man. It took many years, and many life lessons of my own, before I could make sense of his life and see how it fitted into mine, how he became the man I knew.

My mother was not at all like my father; she was not an affectionate woman. Very rarely did I see her embrace my Dad. At best, an inclined head would be offered on his return home from the office while she busied herself with one of her hobbies – either creating a new dress on her sewing machine or piecing together an elaborate giant jigsaw puzzle. He would snap up the morsel and peck her on the cheek. I assumed that my mother didn't love him enough. I assumed my father was weak because he would pander to her every whim. I 'assumed' too much in my little world, and it ate me up.

Like so many marriages that begin full of hope, fuelled by passion, dreams and the mutual desire for eternal happiness, after 29 years my parents separated and divorced.

A few years later, living in eternal but false hope that my mother would return, my father suffered a stroke. His mind was still lucid and sharp, but his body was crippled on one side and his speech slurred and often incoherent. I took him into my home where I looked after him in the hope that he would recover and begin life afresh – as he had done more than once in the past. I dressed him, fed him and bathed him, but he hated it, the loss of dignity.

I told him what he had impressed on me, that if you believe in yourself you can do anything. But the human body is not immortal, and a person can take only so much. He said he didn't want to go on anymore. He had given up, and I needed to respect that.

However, it was there, in that vulnerable state, that he unlocked his heart to me to reveal the man that dwelt within. During those last lonely years I read his military logbook, saw the old black and white photographs taken by the Spitfire's camera when he fired at a target. I sensed his loneliness and felt a tiny bit of the sadness that was at the core of the man that was my father.

I asked him, on a good day, why he had given so much attention to my mom and by comparison, so little to his children.

'You know how your mom loved putting together those jigsaw puzzles, with thousands of little pieces,' he mumbled. 'Well, it's a bit like that. When you buy the puzzle it's usually because you are attracted to the beautiful picture on the box, but also it's because you are excited about the challenge of seeing it become that picture,' he mused, his mind drifting back.

'I pieced my puzzle together – a beautiful home, a beautiful woman and five beautiful children. When the puzzle was complete it looked a lot like the picture I'd had in my mind, but I noticed there was one small piece missing. It's a funny thing,' he continued, 'although things can be near perfect, we tend to see the blemish, the part – no matter how small – that is missing. I tried to find that missing piece in your mother, instead of in myself,' he said, with watery eyes.

'I see now that you saw the attention I gave her as a lack of love for you kids. But I never loved you less. I just yearned for the missing piece of the puzzle that was your mother's affection,' he concluded, with a deep sigh.

I nodded my head gently in understanding and watched as he fell into a deep sleep. I still felt anger inside, but I was not sure why. Alone in my room, I wept properly for the first time since I had left the army. Real sobbing tears. I was sad at many things, but mostly I was sad at the deep loneliness inside myself.

I felt my beautiful, elegant mother didn't really love me, or any of us really, except maybe my brother Marius whom she often referred to as her favourite, until I understood. Unfortunately, I only got that understanding when I was 20 and heard her sad, long-suppressed story for the first time.

My mom was only 13 when her father died. She was the eldest of three children; her younger siblings were twins, a boy and a girl. One day, while playing with them in the garden, she left them briefly and went into the house. On her return, her brother was missing. Her dad, who had suffered from depression for many years, had collected his son in his car and driven to a remote place. There he placed a pipe from the exhaust into the cab and, with the engine running, had taken their lives. In his delusional madness, he murdered his only son.

A few months later my mom was placed in a convent. She felt responsible for her brother's death. She felt blamed by her mother. There was no trauma counselling back then, no-one to lean on, no-one close to love her. She had lost her father; she had lost her brother and now, placed in a convent, felt as though she had lost her mother and sister as well. How does one empathise with such sadness and loneliness? How much and how wrongly I had assumed in those past years. How negatively those assumptions affected me I'm not sure, but maybe it's got something to do with my ability to overcome physical pain. If I've learned anything from that, it's that we should have spoken more as a family – better communication, trust, forgiveness.

The fact that my mother couldn't express her feelings outwardly did not mean for a minute that she didn't have feelings, or felt less. All my mother had done was put her pain inside in order not to have to live with it constantly, and I had misjudged and condemned her for that. Whenever I would think about it later, an all-too-familiar tightness gripped my gut muscles.

And then I'd think of my special, talented brother Marius. We shared a room for more than 15 years. We laughed, fought and shared dreams. We would whisper quietly in the dark so Dad couldn't hear us. He shared how he wanted to be a great artist one day. I told him how the Earth, the 'big animal', was hurting and how too many people were smothering her. We both talked about protecting her. I'd felt so close to him back then. Marius was highly intelligent, bordering on genius, I suspect. Unlike me, though, he had a natural physical ability. From when he was at junior school he won the Victor Ludorum as the top all-round athlete. He rarely trained, he simply went out on the day and won. He was the youngest person at our high school to play in the school's rugby first team.

He was also a non-conformist, a rebel. He struggled to share his deeper emotions and was deeply affected by my parents' divorce. He internalised things and developed an ulcer. Marius found his escape through drugs. Beginning with marijuana, or weed, he never thought it would go any further. 'I'm in control,' he would say. I guess we all feel we're in control and we are, until we're not. The problem is that seldom can we tell when it is that we step over the precipice of no return – and then for most of us it's too late.

I remember going to my mother and telling her that I thought Marius was doing drugs. She wouldn't believe me and actually got angry with me, accusing me of making ridiculous and unfounded accusations. Only when Marius was an adult did my mother accept what he was doing.

I broke away from Marius and his world of addictions by learning the hard lesson of saying no. As the eldest, I tended to rescue my siblings – or try to. I would help them with money on occasions, which usually only helped to fuel bad habits. Instead of empowering them, I can see now I was actually disempowering them by aiding their dependence on people and things other than themselves.

One day I arrived at my home on Signal Hill to find that Marius had moved in with his wife and son. I allowed it for a few days until I heard them fighting. I tried to intervene and realised it was not my place to do so any longer. Something happened to me on that day. I wrote Marius a letter. I told him I loved him, but would no longer support him as long as he was abusive, both to himself and to his family. I asked him to leave and, in my heart, I let him go. He never contacted me again.

Five years later Marius was found lying on a park bench, at the age of 42, dead from a heroin overdose. He was one of the most gifted individuals I've ever known. I still mourn his loss deeply and silently. But mostly I'm angry at the waste of it all.

As I got closer to Beijing, the smog outside must have affected my inner sight and thoughts. It was much darker than it should have been; I felt out of place and I missed my brother very much. I felt heavy and drained from the emotional inner journey I had just lived through, on top of all the emotions unleashed by my meeting with the Wall and all its implications, and I wanted to be alone. Tomorrow will be another day and I'll feel fine, I told myself, unconvincingly. We would spend the night in a hotel in Beijing before heading off into the Gobi desert by train the next day.

5

Storm Warning

EARLY THE NEXT MORNING WE MADE OUR WAY to the old Beijing train station. The place was huge. People everywhere, scurrying about like ants, carrying cheap bags some as large as themselves. After clearing the security check, we boarded the train with William. He had booked a soft-sleeper compartment for the 32-hour journey to Jiayuguan, deep in the north-west Gansu province. This was to be the starting point of our journey when we returned little more than a year later. Being confined to a carriage compartment for so long proved to be very rewarding. It allowed David and me not only to get to know William better but also, with his guidance, to plan a strategy for the expedition.

William had brought food for the long ride. Tea, eggs, pickled cucumbers and noodle soup. The local take-away option was the noodle bars that are popular throughout China. Even in the remotest village you'll find a noodle bar not too far away. Noodles with meat, noodles with tofu, noodles with chillies and sprouts, but always noodles swimming in a fatty broth with oil patterns floating in the steam. Little did I know how important that fat would become and how our lives would come to depend on it.

As the train piped its repetitive, soulful music through the carriages, William shared his intimate knowledge of the Wall and its long history. He spoke of the Chinese people and how best to interact with them. He told us of their ancient and proud culture. (In fact, the Chinese generally feel so apart from and superior to everyone else on the planet and, until recent DNA research revealed otherwise, some Chinese palaeontologists were intent on proving they were descended from an ancestral line different from the rest of humanity.)

We discussed ways of obtaining permits to journey through the nine provinces linked by the Wall, and how we would find food and water in the remote regions.

'Drink only from wells,' he cautioned. 'Dysentery and other diseases are a reality.' 'The support crew will carry loads of bottled water so it's imperative that you try to meet up with them daily if possible,' he said in a serious tone, his eyebrows turned upward towards the centre, creating a furrowed forehead.

William was proving to be invaluable. All the while, my dream was coalescing and becoming ever more material.

The dining car provided an opportunity to meet the locals. Not knowing any Chinese, we relied on William to translate. We were the only foreigners on the train and most of the other passengers were peasant farmers returning home to their rural villages in the Gobi desert. A friendly folk, fascinated by my blond hair, they would gently pull the hairs on my forearms and laugh. This broke the ice and warm *pijou* (beer) was shared.

Jiayuguan is the end of the long snake of rail line heading into the arid Gobi interior. We disembarked and caught a taxi to our very basic hotel. En route I saw a giant billboard showing a row of conservative-looking gentlemen, all dressed in suits, giving a thumbs-up sign. I was intrigued and asked William what the sign said.

'Protect our environment,' he answered with a wry smile.

He explained how China was coming to realise, perhaps too late, how everyone needed to look after our greatest asset if we wanted our children to inherit a hospitable planet. I was amazed that this sort of message was being displayed out here, in the middle of nowhere. I wondered if anybody took heed.

The next morning was another early start. It was so cold our breath formed frosty white crystals in the night air. We climbed into a minute taxi and rattled off into the darkness. Just minutes into the trip and I thought our future expedition was headed for an early demise. On these rural, pot-holed roads just wide enough for one car and maybe a skinny Chinese donkey, you drive in the middle with lights on bright. As another vehicle approaches, also with brights on, it's a game of dare. When both vehicles look destined for a head-on, they swerve sharply onto their respective sides, passing with inches to spare and horns blaring.

After an hour of much blaspheming, at a signal from William, we pulled over. It was still dark. David and I followed William through a few dongas and rough, compacted ground towards a horizon just starting to be defined in the predawn. The crisp smell of an early desert morning, with the air so dense and cold it was almost brittle, was electrifying. I was like a little boy, excited at the big adventure of the day.

A little more than two kilometres further I saw the desert Wall in the coppery first light of the new day. It cast a long, dark, cold shadow on the rough texture of the desert sand. It was totally different in construction to what I had seen in the mountains. Here there was no chiselled stone. Some eight metres high and four metres wide at the base, the Wall was built from the desert sand, straw on occasion, and water. The water would have been transported by thousands of camels carrying their precious cargo in clay urns or pig skins. Layers measuring 10 to 15 centimetres thick were manually compacted using wooden T-shaped stomping blocks.

I climbed a broken, precarious section of the Wall and jogged along the brittle top towards a watchtower; David did not follow my example, as he had a thing about heights and exposure that would test him later. I carefully climbed the barren block of a look-out point, using holes made by birds for foot holds. It was here, standing alone on the exposed point, that I got my first real perspective of the desert Wall and what we would be in for the following year. Looking behind me, the Wall snaked to the horizon and vanished. Just a bronze line framed above by the incredibly blue sky.

Far ahead it crawled over undulating hills towards the far distant snow-covered Black Mountains. I took out my binoculars but all they did was add greater distance to what my own eyes could see. I thought I could anticipate the magnitude of what lay ahead. I tried to imagine looking at those kinds of distances day after day, week after long week, for close on four months. I was excited but also scared. Scared of the pain I knew was waiting, and scared of failing. I wondered if my pride and ego could outlast the Great Wall.

As I stood on the lonely mud tower in the Gobi desert, I knew I needed a cause beyond myself if I wanted this epic journey to end successfully. Wanting an adventure was great, but I knew that pain would offer an ever-present temptation to chuck in the towel. It certainly wasn't going to be a race, more like an undertaking of mental and physical survival. But I wanted it so that I could use the experience to come to know myself better, bring deeper meaning to my life and grow from it.

Proving to myself and to others that nothing is impossible is great, certainly, but it was not enough. There was too much ego for my liking in doing it just for that. I had succeeded in running from Plettenberg Bay to Cape Town some 31 years earlier precisely because I had not done it only for myself. So there and then I decided I would look for a worthy cause.

One that would make for a win-win situation and would compel me to go beyond my own physical pain. It needed to be something powerful enough to drive me forward, knowing I would be benefiting others as I did and that a failure on my part would have potentially grave consequences for others.

As we ran next to the Wall in the warming day, I discussed my thoughts with David. Initially, he was opposed to the idea of raising money for a charity, because he felt it would distract him and he would lose the deep focus needed to complete the journey. I understood how he felt. He needed to put all his energy into training and not be distracted by other business. He thought that getting involved with charities and sponsors would inevitably bring with it media attention and that in turn would lead to further distraction and compromise his chances of succeeding. I suggested we think about it and discuss it when we were back home in South Africa. He said he was fine with that.

We had covered about 30 kilometres. The scenery was monotonous, it was hot and I was bored. My mouth was dry and my tongue stuck to my palate. I wondered how I would be feeling after a month of this bland, dry nothingness. I would find out a year later! I sucked on the hose of my water bladder and got a mouthful of luke-warm water. After swishing the water around to lubricate my mouth, I spat it out. Then I sucked in a second, cooler mouthful and swallowed. I closed my eyes and savoured the sensation of that coolness moving down to my stomach. With my eyes still closed, I thought I heard a strange droning sound somewhere ahead of us.

It didn't fit into this vast, desolate place.

'Sounds like a truck,' said David, and it was.

A foil-like strip shimmered in the midday heat in front of me. It was a tarred road laid out across the desert and which cut through a break in the Wall, as though some giant had slashed the landscape with a knife. William said he wanted to show us something. We stopped in the by now blazing heat. I guessed the temperature was up around 40 °C, and there was no shade.

'Can't he show us later?' I thought impatiently.

He took his rucksack off, laid it on the powdery ochre ground and carefully removed a plastic sleeve. Inside was an old photograph. He pulled it from the sleeve and held it out at arm's length in front of him. Looking over the top of the picture, he looked like a quantity surveyor aiming at some obscure point in the distance.

'Recognise this?' he asked.

I stood next to him and peered at the photograph.

There was a vintage truck on an old tarred road. On the far side of the road was a mud watchtower with the Wall stretching away behind it. I followed William's gaze and realised I was looking at the very same tower on the other side of a now barricaded highway.

'I took this picture more than 20 years ago from exactly this position,' he said, with a hint of nostalgia in his voice. 'This was the area where I was caught and deported,' he continued.

'Although China is still a communist country today, things are more flexible now and foreigners are no longer a novelty or a threat. Although, I must add, in some provinces they are still unwelcome. When I did my journey, things were much stricter and I had to duck and dive to avoid getting caught,' he recalled.

We crossed the barbed-wire fence that lined the road. I wondered why, as only the occasional truck lumbered past every 10 minutes or so. I later learned that there is a 'wall' culture in most of China. This had been passed on through many generations of wall-builders. They seemed to have an incessant need to close themselves in and, indeed, for much of its history China has closed itself off from the outside world. The country's name means 'the inner kingdom' and foreigners – seen to be inferior – have seldom been welcomed in.

Even out here in the middle of the back of beyond, a fence separated the road from the desert. On the far side of the road we entered the shade of a truck-stop, which seemed lonely and totally out of place. This was to be our pick-up point. We sipped *pijou* and waited in the shade of the dirty 'no-horse' town for the next bus. Two hours later we climbed aboard a heaving, sweaty armpit excuse for a bus, wedged ourselves into the hugely overcrowded vehicle and clattered off back to Jiayuguan where the promise of a shower awaited. The people on the bus stared at us unashamedly, their broad smiles showing big silver fillings. Most, if not all of them, had never seen a white person before. We were clearly the best entertainment in weeks!

The next day we spent the morning exploring another section of monotonous mud Wall. I caught a desert agama – a lizard species – and wondered if at any stage on the run the following year I'd be forced to catch things like it in order to eat and stay alive. I put him down and watched as he scurried away to the safety of a hole. Climbing down a gully, I came across some human remains. A femur, a tibia and a piece of a cranium lay bleached white by the sun. I was intrigued and wondered if they were the remnants of a wall-builder of old. In the not-too-distant future, graves and bones would become just part of the landscape.

Back in the hotel by lunch time, we sat around the lazy Susan in the dining room and discussed the way forward with William. He had ordered an array of strange foods and too many litres of *pijou*.

The ritual was simple: if you wanted a sip from the small plastic cup, you needed to look at the person who was in conversation with you, raise your cup and say '*gambey*', meaning 'good health', then down the beer in a few hasty gulps. If, however, someone else wanted a sip and was not in conversation with anyone in particular, he would simply raise his cup, move his arm in a circular motion to the entire table, shout '*gambey*' and everyone would have to chug down their beer. This continued for a good few hours and, needless to say, the child welled up in all of us. We spoke of the great journey we were going to make and how nothing could stop us. But even with all the bravado, there was a tight little knot in my gut.

Although it was only early afternoon, it suddenly got gloomy outside.

'There's a dust storm on the way,' said William.

Within minutes the street lights were on, vehicle lights were on, hooters were blaring and pedestrians were running frantically to find shelter. The storm was being pushed down by strong winds from Mongolia and soon there was no-one on the streets. The air outside the hotel had turned an ominous deep sepia. I could taste the chalky dust even in the insulated hotel. I couldn't believe the speed of it all.

'How could anyone survive out there?' I thought, now substantially more sober. My stomach, which had been loose with beer, tightened again.

'They're death traps,' said William, now very serious. 'Every year people die in these things. That's why you should start in autumn; you don't see these killer storms after summer,' he assured, though not quite reassuringly enough for my liking.

The next morning fine dust lay everywhere, the tarred roads of Jiayuguan looked like dirt roads and the sky still had an eerie pale monochromatic patina. We made our way to the station for the long ride back to Beijing. David and I stood next to the sign painted on the outside of our carriage: 'Beijing–Jiayuguan' it read. We locked hands in friendship and commitment. We really were going to do this thing.

6

The Wild Child is Born

THIS TIME, AS I LAY ON MY BUNK ON THE TRAIN, I felt more positive. William was supporting us, I had seen the daunting terrain but believed I was capable of completing the planned run provided we got all the necessary infrastructure in place. I felt even more strongly about finding a charity to carry with me, and to carry me. As I peered out the window, staring blankly at the desert dunes drifting by, my mind wandered back to the only other long run I had undertaken after my run from Plettenberg Bay to Cape Town at the age of 17. I remembered clearly how the cause came before the run and how important that proved to be.

In 1997 I was an honorary ranger for South African National Parks. Because of my military experience I was appointed as the only parks-accredited para-military instructor providing free services to the SANParks Counter Poaching Unit. This involved training park rangers in disciplines such as weapons handling, bush-lane shooting, fire-and-movement, bush survival and tracking. I joined the Honorary Ranger Corp because I wanted to make a difference to my little corner of the Earth and believed that our game sanctuaries needed protecting at all costs.

The word 'sanctuary' means a place of safety and protection. Yet, even in these special places, animals were being protected by too few rangers with limited resources and were not safe. I had seen a lion in the Kruger National Park with a snare cut deep into his neck, still alive but defenceless as hyenas fed on his hindquarters. I had also seen an elephant, paralysed from a poacher's spinal shot, his tusks hacked out of his head with an axe, his foot slowly scraping at the earth where he lay in his dying throes.

The park needed money to purchase much-needed equipment for their rangers and I wanted to help.

My now ex-wife and still a close friend, Louise (also an honorary ranger), issued the challenge: 'Come on, you can do it again, you're not too old yet!' she taunted. 'Run from Tsitsikamma National Park to Table Mountain National Park, it's only around 600 kays,' she said.

'Only?' I laughed.

'Ja, but you've done it before and you are wiser now,' she pushed. I wasn't so sure if *wise* was an appropriate word.

'More like crazier,' I replied. She knew she had me hooked.

And so it was that in October 1999 I found myself running 620 kilometres from Tsitsikamma National Park to Kirstenbosch Gardens at the foot of the beautiful Table Mountain National Park. We called the project Wild Child – Children for Conservation.

With Louise in charge of logistics, she established a small committee of honorary rangers. My focus was on my training. While the committee organised sponsors, solicited schools' involvement and organised permits to run along freeways, I went to the Sports Science Institute of SA for guidance. I met with Professor Tim Noakes, arguably the top running expert in the world and author of the much acclaimed book, *The Lore of Running*. He referred me to Dr Andrew Bosch, also at the institute, who became my trainer.

He put together a schedule that would mimic the run: one day running, one day talking to schools, one day running, the next day talking to schools. A few weeks before the start date I suffered a calf injury that required me to rest and recover for a few weeks. Andrew, erring on the conservative side, was not convinced I had done enough to pull it off. I had two choices: cancel the whole thing or just do it. I wasn't about to cancel after all the months of effort the committee had put in to make this project come about.

'You can do this thing,' I chided myself. 'For the sake of the animals and the children; make it happen,' I convinced myself.

SAPPI timber and paper company sponsored 1,500 bright yellow T-shirts for kids who would run relay sections with me. It was amazing. As I ran into a town, some 200 youngsters would join me for the last few kilometres, all cheering enthusiastically. The pain became secondary when I met up with these children. They motivated me to keep believing in myself. They still dreamed big dreams and never doubted that I would make it. I certainly wasn't going to let them down.

I met with the 16 mayors of the respective towns I ran through. They all signed a Charter of Interdependence, which was the commitment of their communities to helping their youth work for sustainability with nature.

The support team was usually a day ahead of me, setting up appointments, planning accommodation and putting up the all-important counter-poaching display that the honorary rangers had put together over the years. The display was made up of an array of items: snares, a rhino skull without its horn, a picture of a child holding an orphaned lion cub and framed pictures of lions, antelope and elephants lying in poachers' snares after long and painful deaths. Tragic and sad.

But what saddened me the most was that large shopping malls around Cape Town, where wealthy people shopped, would not allow us to exhibit the display.

'It is offensive and will stop people buying,' I was told by a manager at one shopping mall. 'People don't want to see that stuff,' she insisted.

I was so angry and frustrated at the selfishness and arrogance that seems to pervade our society.

It seems people with the kind of conviction that is needed to stand up and speak out against the ills of the current system are all too rare. Or rather, adults with conviction are rare. I have found that children are much less spoilt by societal norms and conventions and have some kind of beautifully naïve moral compass. They don't care if it's uneconomical to treat animals kindly and to provide for the elderly. They just know it's right. They haven't yet been taught that to run a business, a country or a planet, one has to compromise on those issues. They haven't yet made the acquaintance of our greater god, the god that has governments and whole civilisations spellbound and in its glory outshines all earthly virtues and values: money.

Hence on my 'non-run' days I visited schools and showed children what was happening to our natural resources. Many schools had entered a poster competition we were running. More than 500 posters, offering solutions for sustainability, were collected for display.

Running up the last stretch of road into Kirstenbosch Gardens, I felt like the Pied Piper of Hamelin with something around 400 children in tow, including my son Benjamin who was dressed in our woolly mascot Wild Child costume. At the finish, my old friend James Siddle was there to welcome me. The then Minister of Environmental Affairs, Mr Valli Moosa, was also present.

He said to the public and media gathered in the hall: 'I am here for one reason and one reason only, and that is, from the bottom of my heart and the heart of our government, to thank Braam Malherbe for what one must consider to be a prime patriotic example to not only our children, but to all South Africans.'

I felt privileged to receive such a special message, but all I did was run. The team and the 10,000-plus children who participated were the real heroes.

The next day the local daily newspaper carried a picture with the heading: 'Lone Ranger's Mission Accomplished'. I didn't feel one bit like a lone ranger. I felt like a very proud member of a great team. Together, we had raised R80,000 for equipment for field rangers and created great awareness of the need to conserve our precious wildlife and other natural resources, particularly among young people – the ones who matter most to me.

Back on my bunk, on a train rolling into the Chinese hinterland many years later, I tried to remember the feeling of the pain under my feet after that second long run but I couldn't. I just knew it had hurt a lot and I remembered how I had repeated what I had said after my first run at 17 – 'never again'. The long sweeps of rail line wound tightly as the train snaked between steep cliffs. We had left the desert behind and were entering the toes of the mountains – an arid area we would come to know as the 'dongalands'. The sun had long since gone to bed as we pushed into the night.

So why, I asked myself in the dimly lit compartment, was I now planning something as big as this? I thought about how I felt after the other two runs, after the pain, and I found my answer. Firstly, I had undertaken a challenge, an adventure; and I had succeeded. I had felt fear then also, but the sheer exhilaration of achieving a goal that many had said was crazy and impossible had set alight some potent fuel inside me. It did not make me better than others, but it made me feel great about myself. I thought of it as a greatness of the heart – remember that Johnny Clegg song about looking for the spirit of a great heart? I remember feeling brave, courageous and very fulfilled.

I understood that I would never accept mediocrity in my life, and that too felt good, and right. I would rather have others try to pull me down and alienate me than allow myself to subscribe to a life less fulfilled. I wanted to prove to myself that I had the courage necessary to stand for what I believed in and to do whatever was needed to inspire others to do the same.

And, as importantly, I wanted to give back to this beautiful place that has become the focus of my life, my home, the Earth. Part of my giving back has been to motivate others to do the same. I knew then, on that train in those badlands in a far-off place called China, with absolute certainty that I needed to find a worthwhile charity. Sure, I wanted my own larger-than-life adventure, but even more, I now needed it to be bigger than that. Only by benefiting a greater cause beyond my own egotism, would there be a strong enough motivation to drive me to accomplish something truly remarkable, to push beyond my perceived physical limits.

DANGEROUS DREAMS
Playing with Fire

危險的夢想—玩火

7

Fortune and the Brave

THE FLIGHT BACK TO SOUTH AFRICA was a strange transition from the hazy, almost dream-like world I had experienced in China to the old familiar patterns of home. It was back to reality and lots of logistical planning, not to mention some serious training.

For the second time I broached the subject of a charity with David. He was still reluctant, but a little more open-minded to my reasoning. He still believed it would distract us and felt we should focus only on the goal of running the Wall. I told him I did not want to do this journey only for my benefit and that if I had an incentive that would benefit others, my chances of succeeding would be that much greater. I said I would take on the task of looking for a worthy beneficiary and then we could make an informed decision. He was agreeable to that.

Finding a charity that I believed in and that was credible, with a good record of success and in synch with my own values, was not as easy as you'd think. Personally, my first priority and commitment – as with both my previous long runs – was the natural environment. Unfortunately, nature doesn't buy products, people do. Therefore, finding a sponsor with a corporate social investment policy benefiting people is way easier than finding one aligned to saving the environment.

My second choice would be children – the innocent. They are most in tune with nature and sensitive to the plight of our Earth. They are still part of the instinctual realm. Most adults have extricated themselves from the natural cycle of things and rather try to bend nature to suit them – to our ultimate collective demise. So, for me to find a human beneficiary, I needed it to be a charity that worked with children.

I have found that the more I trust my intuition, the more I realise that coincidence is usually a deceiving veil. After our recce trip to China we produced a DVD to use in our presentations to potential sponsors. I was showing it to my old friend Arn Sylvester and sharing my ideas with him. 'You should show this to Natalie,' he said, 'she would find this interesting.'

'Who's Natalie?' I asked.

Natalie Miller is the director of Operation Smile South Africa. Originally from the USA, she had recently arrived in South Africa to set up Operation Smile in sub-Saharan Africa. She was staying at Arn's house while looking for accommodation in Cape Town. Arn called her into the living room and asked me to show her the DVD. She thought I was crazy, but still loved the idea.

'Do you know where I've been the past few years?' she asked with a grin. 'I set up and ran Operation Smile in China,' she replied before I could answer.

I was gobsmacked. Her task now was to set up Operation Smile's first mission, or group of operations, in South Africa. The scheduled date was to be late 2006 – exactly when we planned to be in China! It was a natural fit.

Operation Smile is a well-established and respected organisation, started about 25 years ago and now operating in some 20 countries. They perform corrective facial surgery on children who are born with facial deformities, predominantly cleft palates and lips. Because of these disfigurements, the children are seen as misfits and usually feel ugly, not only on the outside, but inside as well. They are mostly ostracised and jeered at by other children and therefore usually don't attend school. They struggle to speak and often have difficulty eating. Their self-esteem is low and sometimes non-existent. Operation Smile changes their lives forever, 'one smile at a time' as their motto goes.

It was the beginning of a long, positive relationship between me and Operation Smile.

Now, with a credible beneficiary in place and William having agreed to be our logistics man in China, we began the hard yards of physical training and finding a sponsor.

Believing in yourself and your dream is one thing, but expecting others to believe in you and your dream – and helping to finance it – is a totally different story. The expedition was not exactly an investor's dream: David and I were pretty much unknown as marketable brands, we lacked credibility and could not boast any 'extreme adventurers' CVs. The project wasn't local – it was virtually on the other side of the planet – and, rather significantly, it had never been done before. What exactly made us so special to believe that we could do it?

Trying to convince a potential sponsor that this was sane, do-able and a sound investment proved to be a huge challenge. With literally hundreds of doors closed in our faces, we sat around a table to discuss the next step.

Time was running out. The harsh reality had to be confronted: were we going to do it, irrespective of whether or not we had a sponsor? David and I were having a meeting at Geoffrey Smith's house.

Geoff was to be our logistics man in South Africa.

'It's your call guys,' he said.

I thought of my dream and that familiar knot in my stomach returned. David said he wanted to go, 'no matter what'. His commitment was contagious.

'Okay, let's go,' I finally replied. We stood up and shook hands. The contract was sealed.

Crazy? To some, perhaps. To me, no. I lay in bed that night, staring at the black depths of space in my starless ceiling, knowing I was going, no matter what. But the tension in my solar plexus was now excitement, not fear.

Somehow, when you have the faith and take the steps towards it, the solutions come. Often more quickly than you could have imagined. We had sealed our commitment on the Wednesday. On Thursday, Jerome Smith, a regular client at David's restaurant, was entertaining guests over lunch (David might not have been an ultra-sports star at the time but he was a well-known and successful restaurateur around Cape Town). Seeing David, he asked if we were still going to China.

'Yes, we leave in six weeks,' David answered.

'Great, who's sponsoring you?' asked Jerome.

'We haven't been able to find a sponsor, so we're going without one.'

I believe that what happened next was the result of faith we had invested in the project, not coincidence.

'I've got a gut feeling that this is going to work,' Jerome said. 'Give me something to write on.'

On a serviette, he wrote and signed a promissory note to be our headline sponsor for the Great Wall Challenge, later to be called the Cipla Miles for Smiles Great Wall Challenge. Jerome is the CEO of Cipla Medpro (now just Cipla), a huge generic pharmaceutical company based in South Africa.

My dad had once told me a definition of faith and I had not forgotten it: 'Faith is to believe something you do not yet see. The result of that faith is to see what you believed.' It works. I had held my dream steadfast and took a courageous decision to pursue it when no-one else believed in me.

They say fortune smiles on the brave.

8

The First Setback

THROUGHOUT OUR RELENTLESS EFFORTS to raise sponsorships, I had to believe it was all going to happen as planned. In this regard I 'ran my talk' daily. Once again I approached Dr Andrew Bosch at the Sports Science Institute, which is located between the SA Breweries plant and Newlands rugby stadium in Cape Town's leafy southern suburbs. He carefully worked out a training plan for me based on the timeline leading up to our scheduled departure date of July 2006.

'This time round,' stressed Andrew, with his almost permanent smile, 'it's going to be a whole different ball game.'

I was to begin the long programme by running 15 kilometres a day, 90 per cent of it off-road on the slopes of Table Mountain, for approximately a month. After that, I was to build up to running 15 kilometres every morning and another 15 kilometres every evening, six days a week. Finally, starting two months before departing for China, I was to do a 15 kilometre morning run, a 15 kilometre lunch time run and a 15 kilometre evening run.

The plan was to try to simulate what I was going to be doing in China. This would maximise my chances of success. It is, of course, difficult to simulate the 30 °C conditions of the Gobi desert in autumn during a wet Cape winter. Equally, I had never experienced −5 °C, let alone the −20 °C we could likely encounter in the Chinese mountains. In simulating the high mountains north of Beijing, I would run up and down Table Mountain (Cape Town's popular tourist destination, at a height of 1,000 m). I would do this four times a week as one of the daily 15 kilometre training sessions.

Then disaster struck. I injured myself only a few months prior to the scheduled start in August 2006 in China. I had already undergone minor knee surgery where a torn meniscus in my right knee had been cleaned up. Dr Willem van der Merwe, my surgeon, had warned me of excessive training. I sought Andrew's advice. He shook his head and calmly but clearly expressed his scepticism.

'I don't think you've done enough to pull this off,' he said.

Although he was giving a purely medical perspective and did not want to break my spirit in any way, I chose to reject his view.

'No-one knows my body like I do,' I thought defiantly. 'I heal quickly and I am positive,' I tried to convince myself, feeling that all-too-familiar anxious tightening in my stomach.

Tim Noakes had often spoken about over-training. After training on the Grucox machine one morning (more of this beast later), we bumped into Tim in the passage. After hearing about how much training David had done, Tim concluded: 'Go, you should be there already, what are you waiting for? Remember, you've still got 3,500 kilometres ahead of you!'

We still had two months before leaving South Africa. I hoped he was right but in my heart I knew that, out of physical necessity, I had hopelessly under-trained.

We were contacted by the media and asked to do a TV interview with Professor Noakes and Professor Wayne Derman at the Sports Science Institute. We were filmed training on the Grucox machines and then the interviews began.

Our physician, Professor Wayne Derman, was asked for his opinion: 'These guys are really committed,' he said. 'If they get through this thing, it's because of their heads. Their bodies are strong but their minds are stronger,' he continued, with that look I had gotten to know so well – slightly mischievous but with the greatest sincerity.

Then Tim was asked for his opinion: 'I think it's highly improbable that they will complete the event. For the reason that they are trying to run a marathon every day for more than 100 days. In fact, the last time that something like this was attempted, was when Scott walked to the South Pole with his team in 1911/12. They man-hauled, 10 hours a day, for 159 days and we calculated they expended about a million calories, and that, to our knowledge, is the greatest human performance ever.

'The difference here is that these guys are actually running; they're running on difficult surfaces, and they're running at different altitudes in different environmental conditions. So, in my opinion, this is physically impossible. The probability that something unforeseen will happen during the event that will prevent them from completing is so high, that the probability of their success is essentially zero.'

Hearing Tim say those words was not particularly encouraging. He is, after all, arguably the world's leading expert on these matters. I had known

Tim for some years and knew that he had come around to believing the difference between those who achieved their goals and those who didn't was usually in their heads. I also knew I had heard those words before: 'it's impossible'. In the past I had chosen to ignore them and I had succeeded. Tim had inadvertently done me a favour; he had thrown down a gauntlet before me. At that late stage in my preparation, I could not allow a single seed of doubt to enter my consciousness, so I accepted the challenge, like a duel to the death, deep inside myself.

I visited my friends Cathy Chambers and Sean Surmon at the Health Junction. Cathy, in my opinion, is one of the top sports physiotherapists around. Thorough and deeply sincere, Sean is a biokineticist and had already helped me with various proprioception exercises – helping to give feedback on the body's internal working. They went to work on me immediately and I was soon back on the mountain – but still nowhere close to my planned schedule. I continued as best I could, always remaining positive.

Training for an expedition of this magnitude is not only physical exercise. As my dietician and friend Shelly Meltzer pointed out: 'What you put into your body is vital. We need to find out what's available in the isolated areas of rural China,' she said. 'If you don't put the right stuff into your body, your chances of survival, let alone finishing, will be severely compromised.'

She sent sample menus containing the correct protein, carbohydrate and fat balances to William in China.

Calories and mineral content were examined.

'What vegetables could be sourced in the Gobi desert?' she pushed us to get this side of things right. 'What about the high mountains and the cold? How often will you get fresh food? What about fresh water?' she drilled down into the issue.

At that stage I had no idea, but with her astute prompting we found out and we found solutions. A big concern of Shelly's (and mine) was that without the correct nutritional intake, my immune system could collapse. Shelly analysed various vitamin and mineral supplements from our naming sponsor Cipla, as well as protein and carbohydrate supplements. Eventually, after testing various products in training, the correct combinations became part of my daily diet.

Training became even more scientific. As part of the rehab programme after my meniscus operation, Dr Willem van der Merwe introduced me to a mechanical invention of his called the Grucox device. It looked something like a customised spinning bike, with a keypad and computer screen; it pedals backwards though, at a speed and torque based on data input. It is essentially an eccentric training device designed to strengthen and build the stabilising muscles around the knee joints, even going as far as to elasticise the associated tendons. I spent many hours on The Blue Beast, as David aptly called it. The results were outstanding and my legs strengthened incredibly, especially my quads, with a definite increase in muscle density.

Not only was physical preparation required, but also mental: not so much my personal mental attitude, but more in terms of team dynamics. We needed to know how to resolve the stress that would inevitably develop between us when we became physically and mentally drained and how we would best work as a team of people from different countries and cultures. David and I have very different personalities and I wanted this to be an asset, not a liability. I felt it was vital that together we consult with a sports psychologist, someone who understood team dynamics when physical demands were consistently high. Again the Sports Science Institute provided the man: Clinton Gähwiler, who comes across as a very unassuming guy but is highly intelligent and astute in his ability to assess situations. He was able to offer positive opportunities for us to explore during our run and grow through them. He explained to us our personality differences so that we could learn to complement each other and avoid unnecessary conflict.

As humans, without this understanding, we often compete instead of complement. This is especially true of men, where ego (and testosterone) tends to take over when challenges present themselves or conflict arises. As long as we push to try to get the other person to accept our point of view, how can we honestly see theirs? As long as we do this, we stunt our own growth. Being convincing does not necessarily mean you're right. David and I each needed to be an asset to the other. We were going to be together under extreme physical and mental stress for a long time. Clinton helped me see the necessity to appreciate differences as assets.

'Two heads are better than one,' he said, 'as long as you value each other's opinions.'

Clinton gave David and me some tests to complete. The results showed David to be more of an amiable personality, but with a strong will. He would stick to his guns, sometimes obstinately, yet did not like confrontation and would tend to dismiss issues and close up. I was shown to be more 'driver' or task orientated, with a tendency to express my opinion easily. Sometimes too easily.

David would need to open up more and be more flexible to sometimes accept my opinion or the opinion of others. On the other hand, I would have to shut up more and be a better listener. If David appeared sullen, I would need to give him space and time before confronting him. I also needed to understand that if he was non-communicative, the cause was not necessarily me. On the other hand, I needed to be able to say what I felt without David taking it personally. It would be interesting, in the months ahead, in a strange land, with a diverse team, to see how personal differences would provide an opportunity for growth for all of us.

The days moved by too quickly. Suddenly we were sorting through the heaps of gear sponsored by Adidas. There were three different types of shoes: off-road trail shoes, softer shoes for gravel roads and hard-soled shoes for the mountains and the snow. They were Gore-Tex lined for warmth and waterproofing. Then the expedition gear: shorts, vests, second skins, leggings, gloves, windbreakers, down jackets ... literally piles of stuff.

'Heck,' I thought 'where am I going to pack all this stuff?' My lounge floor looked like a clothing store on stock-taking day.

9

The Letter

WHILE I WAS PACKING, A TENSION DEVELOPED in me that had unpleasant manifestations for those around me at the time; I was short-tempered and snapped at those closest to me. I expected everyone to understand my feelings, yet I had little regard for theirs. How could anyone else understand when I hardly could? At night I dreamed of deserts. I had nightmares of being trapped in a sand storm: I couldn't see; I could only hear a noise that sounded like jet engines; and I couldn't breathe. I'd wake up gasping for air. The nightmare kept recurring for about two weeks in different forms.

Once, in one of these dreams I was back in the old hotel in Jiayuguan, thankful that I was watching the chalky dust outside from the safety of the hotel. Then, suddenly, the hotel vanished and I was alone in the storm, lost and pathetic, knowing I was going to die. Everything went into slow motion. Then I woke up, gasping for air. The Wall was real, tangible, inside me every night. In the days before leaving I was excited much of the time. Waking in the dark of night, I was often petrified. How the darkness plays tricks on the mind.

It was an extremely emotional period – especially for my girlfriend at the time, Mandi, who stood by me through thick and thin and is now a special friend. I will always love her and am eternally grateful for her support during that period of my life. It was maybe even tougher for my son Benjamin. I had no idea what he was going through. I knew he was scared, but he put up a brave front, always trying to understand and be supportive.

The two of them were at the sharp end of my tension. The situation I was getting myself into had massive risks attached, death among them. And that had to be dealt with. I signed power of attorney to my dear and close friend Belinda. I asked Benjamin, only 17 at the time, if I died, who would he choose as a dad. A hard question and a painful one for both of us. 'Mac,' he said in his gentle, soulful way. 'I would want to be with Mac.'

I had no idea what I was putting my son through until much later.

I called Ian MacPherson, 'Mac', and asked if we could meet.

Mac had lost his only son Lloyd in a tragic down-hill skateboarding competition only two years earlier. Ben had introduced Lloyd to the sport and was present at the hospital, holding his best friend's hand, when the life-support system was switched off. Ben and Lloyd considered each other as brothers. Mac listened to me, agreed, and the papers were signed.

Then suddenly it was time to leave. I walked around my home on the rump of Signal Hill. I strolled through the garden, not wanting to leave but anxious to get going at the same time. That moment had taken so long to come around. I hugged my beautiful German shepherds, Max and Buena, and could feel they had picked up the tension. I didn't realise then just how much I would miss them on those cold walls, high in the windy mountains.

During emotional goodbyes at Cape Town International Airport, Ben gave me a sealed envelope. 'Please don't open it until you're on the plane,' he said as we hugged each other.

'I love you so much,' I said. It was somewhere over the Indian Ocean, en route to China via Singapore, that I read his letter:

Dear Dad

I know I haven't really shown you how proud I am of you on this whole journey. I think it's because I am scared, sad, angry, happy for you, worried, anxious. There are so many feelings happening. I am scared that something will happen. I am angry that I won't see you for so long.

But most importantly I am happy for you. I think that this journey will teach you things. I am happy because every day you will be in nature. I am happy because you have a close friend with you. I am happy because you can meet with your inner self. I am happy because there will be silence and time to think. I am happy because your journey has a _real_ reason: YOU MUST BE HAPPY.

Dad, please don't even think about ever giving up because you can do it. Don't stress, be happy.

Remember every step you take is one step closer to home and the people that love you.

I am so proud of you, not just for what you are doing but because you are my dad.

I really really am proud of you. Please try not to lose my lucky stone. I

*believe in it. Keep it with you and when you touch it remember how much
you have to be grateful for. I love you so much.*

*You are always in my thoughts and in my dreams. I love you Dad and am
so proud. Good luck. God bless!*

*Love you lots and always will
Benjamin*

It was the longest flight of my life. I had tears in my eyes and just wanted
to talk to him, to tell him again how much I loved him, to hold him tight,
to never let him go. I called him from Singapore. He told me not to worry,
that it would all work out fine. The son often teaches the father if he will
only listen.

After exiting customs at Beijing airport, I looked at the huge mural of
the Great Wall for the second time. It appeared mystical, like an illusion,
as mist and cloud danced amongst its silent, lonely towers. Forewarned
by our recce trip more than a year earlier, I knew that before I was to see
and feel those cold stone watchtowers again, we needed to cross the Gobi
desert. It would be at least two months away.

We met William at our hotel where he informed us that Hans and Michael,
our two Austrian friends, and part of the support team, would be arriving
the next day. Although David and I were going to be doing the hard yards
each day, we both knew the value and importance of a good support crew.
The two Austrians, Hans Seer and Michael Rainier, were vital to the success of the expedition.

Hans and David had been friends for many years. Hans and his wife Inga
managed a ski resort and *Berghaus* in the small Austrian town of Leogang.
I first met them in 2002 when I'd joined David on my first skiing holiday.
Hans and I got on immediately. The way he welcomed me and accepted me
so openly set the foundation for a long friendship. Hans had been a soldier
in the Austrian military for many years. He is physically strong and accus-
tomed to hard work. Also, he's a talented musician and part of a popular
band in the town. When David suggested Hans join us as our logistics and
cameraman in China, I agreed immediately.

Michael? I had met him once briefly in Cape Town some years earlier.
He's a medical doctor well experienced in mountain rescue in the Austrian
Alps. In stature he is not a big man, like Hans, but he is solid and in his

heart he's a lion. He's very focused, with a gentle sense of humour, and also an excellent musician. He was duly appointed our team doctor in China.

A noble point here: there was not sufficient money in our sponsorship for salaries for David and me. Due to unforeseen but vital miscellaneous items that needed to be purchased, Hans and Michael agreed to be part of the expedition without any remuneration. It was testament to their level of commitment. Even back home people had shown by deeds and actions how much they believed in us. When friends Hugh and Shelly Knevit heard that money was tight, their gift was my return air ticket.

Part of William's mandate was to put together the Chinese support crew. The team consisted of six people, all of whom William knew and had worked with before to a greater or lesser degree. The head of the Chinese team was Lunga, which means 'dragon'. In many respects the name suited him: a tall, strong man, he had a commanding presence.

Piou, our interpreter, was a young, intelligent academic fellow, originally from South Korea. As the only member of the Chinese team who could speak English, we relied on him for clear and open communication. I had no idea how important this was to be in the months that lay ahead!

Lilly was our beloved cook. We had met before on the recce trip at William's farmhouse in the mountains. I needed no convincing as to her culinary skills. William expressed his concern about Lilly being the only woman on the team, but Lunga agreed to be surrogate father to Lilly. He would watch over her and ensure her safety.

Changa, Chang and Lee were employed as camp hands, drivers and guides. These three special men, who each found their way into my heart, were gentlemen who were always polite and always smiled. In fact, by the time we arrived in the country, the Chinese team was already on the road, driving the vehicles along the slow, long and winding road to the start at Jiayuguan. We would meet up with them 10 days later at the end of our train journey into the desert.

This time I experienced the train trip in a completely different light: I stared out of the window, listening to the old familiar *clickety-clack, clickety-clack* as the train wound its way through the mountain gorges, knowing that I would be coming back along the top of those high, silent ridges. As I dozed on the top bunk, waking regularly in the long night, I thought I could feel how far we had to go and it scared the hell out of me. In the morning I looked out at the sprawling desert. It was so desolate, harsh and lonely.

'One day at a time,' I said to myself, repeating it like the mantra of a Buddhist pilgrim.

Later it would become the very mantra that carried me through: 'Just one day at a time, you can do this, you can do this.'

I was reading the book *Between a Rock and a Hard Place*. It was the gutsy story of Aron Ralston, a young American climber who was out exploring the Colorado canyonlands alone when he'd fallen in a narrow gully, dislodged a large boulder and trapped his arm under a 350 kilogram granite block. After five days of hoping and waiting to be rescued, with his food and water depleted, he finally realised no-one knew where he was and help would not be coming. He was alone and would just have to help himself. He used his blunt multi-tool (he had blunted the blade trying to chip the rock away) to hack his trapped arm off. He had no anaesthetic, only the will to survive. In a state of dehydration and utter exhaustion, and risking bleeding to death, he made his way to safety and finally to hospital. But that ordeal had not stopped him climbing: he had a false arm fitted, with an ice axe-like appendage for a hand. Since then he's become a serious high-altitude mountaineer.

It is a story of tenacity and the strength of the human spirit to overcome any obstacle. It inspired me and put me emotionally back on track. In such extreme situations you survive minute by minute, one day at a time, and that was how I was going to do it.

10

Ground Zero

AFTER MORE THAN THREE YEARS OF DREAMING and planning, the day had finally arrived: this one day, this first day of a long journey. Although David was with me, I felt very alone. The morning was getting on and it was getting hot, yet I felt a cold shiver run through me and the hair on my neck prickled. Even with all my knowledge and powers of logic, it all felt not quite real: I felt a little crazy and out of touch, as though I had been slipped some hallucinatory drug. Or perhaps, I thought to myself, this is as real as it's going to get!

The start date had been delayed because some of our medical equipment had got stuck in customs. It was now 24 August 2006, a whole two weeks later than planned, but we couldn't delay the oncoming weather that was the crux of our ground-breaking attempt. Even before we'd begun, the pressure was on us to make up time. I didn't like it one bit. As I stared around me at the most barren, hot, harsh landscape imaginable, I felt surreal, as though in a dream. I looked at the distant mountains.

'I'm going there,' I said to myself in a whisper. I focused on them intently: 'I'm going there,' I repeated.

The Chinese media was interviewing David and me. The time dragged on. It was past midday and hot, not exactly the early start we'd planned. I felt as though I was kneeling in the starting blocks at the beginning of a 100-metre sprint but the gun just never cracked. My stomach was tense, I just wanted to go.

Finally, it was time. We had filled a bottle with water from the Great White River to signify the start of our journey. After writing the GPS co-ordinates on it and placing it carefully in my pack, with arms raised high, I ran my first tentative steps into the unforgiving Gobi desert. It felt good to be moving at last.

The start point at Jiayuguan lay in a wide, uneven and stony plain known as the Hexi (pronounced 'hershi') Corridor. The plain is flanked by the white-tipped Qilian and Black mountain ranges. Even in the burning height of summer, where the valley floor reaches a scorching 50 °C, the mountains still boasted their mantle of snow. The word 'guan' means pass, or passage, and it was here, at the great fort of Jiayuguan, that the legendary Marco Polo and the many other traders and merchants before and after had been granted entry into China's north-west region to trade or to sell their skills.

We had run just over four kilometres when I saw the fort. It seemed suspended on a silver, shimmering mirage, almost as though it was floating on water. The fort was a mere seven kilometres away from the start of the Wall, with its tiny mud watchtower perched precariously on the cliff above the Great White River. With each step the fort loomed ever bigger. With only a few hundred metres of Wall in front of me, I was amazed at the sheer size of the structure. The Wall merged with the western face of the fort.

David and I slowed to a gentle jog and entered the dark entrance from the Inner Mongolia side. As I walked through the arched tunnel I noticed the large cobbled stones, each about the size of a small breadboard. There were grooves worn into the stones from the thousands of carts that had carried their precious cargoes into China. The tunnel was about 30 metres long and at least six metres high at the top of the arch. I felt like just sitting there because the desert air was blissfully cool as it funnelled through the hollow.

On entering the outer courtyard I felt like a dwarf as I stared at the compacted clay faces that towered around me. The fort is now a museum and tourist attraction to those interested enough to make the long, arduous journey to this remote region. It's sheer size would have been a huge deterrent to any invading Mongol army. The Hexi Corridor is a natural break in an otherwise unbreachable landscape.

The Black and Qilian mountains are virtually impenetrable because of their lofty, snow-capped and rocky crags. This is why the Chinese emperors of so long ago decided to build such a massive and impressive fort right across that stretch of Inner Mongolia. David and I climbed the narrow steps to a corner battlement where we could get a clearer view of the day ahead. Looking at the Wall leaving the mighty fort at Jiayuguan and running like a serpent into the distance as far as I could see, I suggested to David we 'put foot'.

Exiting through the cool corridor we ran past the imposing ochre mud walls on our way eastwards. I glanced up at the ornately decorated roofs. I could almost feel the soldiers of long ago on the battlements high above me staring at two crazy guys in vests and shorts running off into nowhere.

But I could not dream for long as there was no time to linger there. We had places to go in a hurry and much precious time to make up. With the fortress shrinking into the horizon behind me, I picked up an SMS from Lunga giving the GPS co-ordinates of our overnight stop. The team was only eight kilometres ahead. Because of our late start we'd managed to cover only 20 kilometres that day. That would have to change if we wanted to reach the high mountains before winter really set in.

That first night we camped out in the remnants of another old, but much smaller fort. As the sun was setting in the west, I climbed the broken stairs to the battlements at sunset and looked east, following the line of broken, mud Wall as it curved like a sun-dried millipede, its segments separated by years of relentless wind. Then it vanished into the rocky, barren foothills of the distant mountains: I was looking into my tomorrow, and countless tomorrows after that.

I went to sleep in my tiny tent thinking of too many things, my mind filled with senseless clutter as I drifted to another place and time.

DESERT PLAINS
Dreams and Nightmares

沙漠地帶——美夢與噩夢

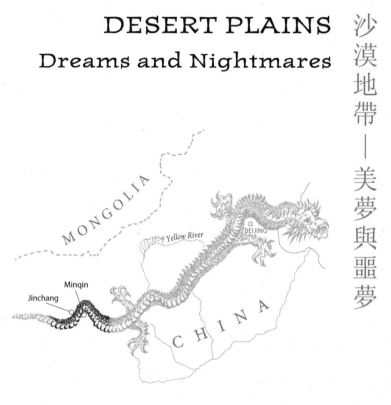

11

Intuition

I DREAMED VIVIDLY THAT FIRST NIGHT in the desert. I dreamed of the first time I had really been alone. Away from people, with only nature around me. Then the wind woke me in the night and I realised where I was. I didn't want to be there, nor did I want the dream I was having of something that had happened long before to continue. I wanted something familiar, more recent and comforting, to dwell on. I tried to dream of my home on the rim of the Cape Town city bowl on a sunny day, of myself lying by the pool with the French doors wide open and Deacon Blue's 'Dignity' playing in the background. I tried to picture my beautiful German shepherds lying on the lawn. It didn't work. When sleep finally took over, the old dream returned.

I had run away from home when I was just 14 years old. Not just down to the corner and then back home for supper, and not because I didn't love my parents, because I did, but because I had watched the movie *Tom Sawyer*. Something about that movie worked its way like a parasitic worm into my imagination. Tom and his mate, Huck Finn, had gone away fishing down the big river. They slept out under the stars, living their adventure. His mom was furious and spoke of the beating he would receive on his return home. But his dad said something that touched my heart: 'Let him be, he will only be a boy once.'

I didn't want to miss out on that – a boy's adventure. I didn't want to be a man one day and have to look back on my life and regret not having known what it felt like to be alone and vulnerable in the great unknown. Thinking about turning the idea into reality frightened me, but it also excited me even more. I wanted to know if I could survive on my own. I think that even back then I knew that if I could, I would feel closer to nature and respect it more.

For a week I planned my big adventure. Little by little I filled my green Bergens H-frame rucksack with tins of food, oranges, biscuits, anything I could pilfer from the pantry without it being noticed. I kept my rucksack and a blue sleeping bag in the storeroom behind our garage. The night before my 'escape' I asked Mom and Dad if I could sleep under the gazebo next to the pool as I often did on summer nights. Lying there awake in the garden, I let the night ghosts into my mind. I was frightened, very frightened.

I had left the letter I had written next to the telephone, telling my folks I would be home in five days but that I would be safe and that I loved them very much.

I don't think I slept much and, when I did, my sleep was restless. When I woke in the predawn I thought of quitting right then.

'What am I doing?' I asked myself. 'What am I trying to prove?' Answers didn't come to me. Then, 'I'm just being a chicken,' I told myself as I quietly put on my rucksack. I wasn't at all convinced about this great adventure thing as I slowly walked down the driveway towards I still wasn't sure exactly what.

When you're that young you tend to miss out a few of the planning details, like where you are actually going. But I didn't think much more about it, I just walked, moving slowly in the darkness from my home in Pinelands towards the suburb of Mowbray. Without thinking consciously about it, I was heading towards the most natural of natural places, and one more than big enough for a boy's big adventure. I hadn't walked a kilometre and the weight of my pack was already unbearable. I tossed some of the cans on a bench at a bus stop and shuffled on.

The cold, fresh smell of the early grey morning left a strange, almost metallic taste in my mouth. I ran my tongue over my palate, trying to rub the taste away. I felt more than just a little bit scared. Even to this day, that smell and taste make me feel uncomfortable, skittish.

Walking over the Black River and the N2 freeway bridge, I thought the lights of every car could be a police vehicle and that they would stop and take me home. Anyone seeing a young boy of 14, walking with a rucksack almost as big as himself, in the dark, on a week day, would surely be suspicious. But no-one stopped me.

I started the long ascent through Mowbray towards the mountain and crossed the footbridge over the last road before heading into the pine forest at the base of Devil's Peak. I turned around and looked at the lights over the Cape Flats and the orange haze signalling the approaching dawn. Then I turned my back on the lights and began lumbering up the hill and into the pine trees.

Passing the imposing granite statue and classical mausoleum of Rhodes

Memorial, on the lower slope of the mountain, I watched the sun rise over the saw-toothed Hottentots Holland mountains into a cloudless pale blue sky. From there I could see where my house was and for a moment I worried about my parents and how frantic they would be, at about that time reading the letter I had written. It's only now, many years later when I am myself a father, that I can really understand the anxiety I must have caused them.

My destination was the King's Blockhouse, an old observation and signalling fort on a ridge overlooking the bay and harbour to the one side and the Cape Flats and southern suburbs to the other, with the far mountains brooding ever over them. It was there, hiding in the shade of the thick stone walls, that I knew for sure for the first time, even through my fear, that every boy needed an adventure to truly live and become a fully formed man.

I spent the days writing poetry and studying insects under rocks and in bushes. I had done this for as long as I could remember, getting my hands dirty turning over rocks and being fascinated by the creatures that lay beneath them. Under one large rock next to the blockhouse, I found a small, harmless brown snake – commonly known as a slug-eater – living in harmony with a striped mouse and a large baboon spider. They lived in comfort under the rock in their refuge of dark silence. Ordinarily, a spider, a mouse and a snake would not share the same space; in fact they would be mortal enemies. But here, where the rock met the soil, a sanctuary of common ground provided a communal home for them. I looked down at the urban sprawl on the flats below. I could hear the continuous humming of the city.

'If natural creatures can share and work together, why can't we?' I wrote in my journal.

One night, lying under a large *waboom* (a type of protea tree), tucked into my sleeping bag and using my rucksack as a pillow, I heard a loud scratching sound close to my head. It was dark and I lay frozen, not daring to move and very frightened. I remember praying and asking God to protect me and that I was *really* sorry for running away and would *never* do anything like that again. It sounded as if something, or someone, was trying to get into my rucksack only centimetres away. My torch was next to my head. I thought if I grabbed it I could hit him or it with the torch; I hardly breathed.

After I don't know how long, I decided to lunge for the torch. I switched it on and looked straight at the most beautiful spotted genet just half a metre away. It was as startled as I was and after a second or two it bolted for safety. I couldn't believe that I could have been so scared of something so small and so beautiful. Somehow, my bargaining with God earlier seemed a little stupid. The time came to leave the mountain and wend my sheepish way home.

I received my deserved punishment when I got home, but I would never have done it any differently. There are some things you just know need to be done.

Using my intuition was something I learned on that mountain as a young boy. I firmly believe I was meant to have been alone in the wilderness at that young age, like training unwittingly for the life that would follow. It was something special that I cherish deeply today still. Being close to nature, confronting and overcoming fear, I have never felt more alive.

Now, waking in the crisp desert morning with the dream still fresh and real, I knew I needed to trust my intuition more than ever. Sure, we had to plan each day ahead and we needed to bond as a team and talk openly about feelings and ideas. But out there, surrounded by the rawness of nature in the Gobi desert, I also had to read the signs around me and trust my gut feelings.

I had learned long ago that to ignore the little voice inside me can be very dangerous. On that second day of the run I vowed to pay close attention to my intuition. In the weeks ahead we would be confronted by situations that made a mockery of clear logic and careful planning. Then I would really appreciate how vital my training to rely on my own intuition would be. I'm convinced it saved my life more than once.

12

One Step at a Time

THE DAYS WERE SERIOUSLY HOT that first week. A dry heat dictated a slow pace. It was a good thing in hindsight, as our bodies and minds were adjusting to the many changes of this new life.

The average day started at first light with Lunga shaking my tent. During that first week I was usually already awake, lying quietly in my cocoon, thinking of the day ahead – psyching myself into a positive mind space. Smear Vaseline on chafe areas: armpits, between my legs and toes. Dress. Pack running bag. Get out of tent. Wash when spare water was available; take a spade and go for a toilet walk. Eat. Our food was to vary dramatically as the journey progressed, but in those first weeks breakfast usually consisted of porridge, eggs, coffee and, occasionally, rusks. Set Garmin (as our GPSs became affectionately known). Go. That whole routine took no more than 30 minutes.

The first six days we'd walk the first kilometre or two in silence to warm up, then run to the 15 kilometre mark, have a health bar, then on to the 30 kilometre mark where we would meet the support crew or, when they couldn't reach us, eat our lunch packs alone before continuing to the day's end point that had been SMSed to us as GPS co-ordinates. Our run packs had two-litre water bladders, so if we thought we might not be able to rendezvous with the crew, we usually put in two extra 500-ml bottles each.

We also carried EAS energy bars and carbohydrate booster sachets. We each carried a 10-metre length of 4-mm thick safety rope, as well as a small medical kit that included an emergency foil blanket. Out of habit, I always had a compass and small binoculars packed. This proved very useful later.

Garmin in South Africa had also supplied us with an A4-size solar panel with a variety of connections. The panel folded to a neat 8×22 cm and was only 5 cm thick, including the battery. We used to strap the panel on one of our back packs and charge cell phones or GPS when necessary. It became an indispensable part of our kit.

During our first week in the 'boonies' there was quite a bit of pent-up tension as we settled into a daily pattern. We usually dealt with it by telling really lame jokes, or with hectically crude comments. Typical boys' stuff. We were in the back of beyond and it didn't take long for the primitive side of our male natures to surface.

At the end of our first week we had clocked just over 230 kilometres. It should have been 250. I wasn't the least bit concerned, but David was. He pointed out that if we also did 15 kilometres less than planned the following week, we would then be 30 kilometres down. Eventually a day, then two, then three behind. We were already two weeks behind schedule, given our late start. But I still felt it was better to err on the side of caution. Start slower, get into things, build our fitness and pick up distance later.

To be honest it also suited my lack of training! Of course we were each right in our own way. But what was more important was that we worked things out together without allowing tension to build. That would be a far greater problem than the one we already had. Already, after only one week on the trot, there was disagreement: we could follow only one regimen but we were pulling in two different directions and I felt the beginnings of stress building.

Lunga suggested we drive to the small town of Xi'an for our first rest day. We all agreed on that at least! Maybe we'd find hot water and even cold *pijou*.

That night our spirits were buoyed up. We all celebrated by staying in a very basic hotel and having pretty good food around the lazy Susan.

'One week down, only 16 to go!' joked Hans.

I didn't find it quite so amusing.

The following day I spent writing the first of many blogs for our website. The blogs were sent from a laptop using a 3G card via our Vodacom international roaming system, back to our website that was used to drum up support and sponsorship for Operation Smile. Mobile phone signals are used for the party bosses in China to communicate with even the most remote village, and we could get a signal just about anywhere; when we couldn't, we were in deep valleys or knew we were near a military area. Those blogs later become the skeleton of the book I finally started to write some three years later. It was while re-reading my blogs, in fact, that the idea to write this book took hold. This is how it began:

After years of dreaming, planning, training and unusually high stress levels, David and I are on the second and more significant part of our journey.

The first part of this journey, for me, was the mental and spiritual preparation. The belief in one's ability to achieve something of this magnitude is a prerequisite to its success. Also, leaving my home and loved ones for such a lengthy period needed careful evaluation of my priorities. We can die in a car accident tomorrow, yet somehow don't believe it will happen. But attempting to cover such a long distance on foot, in harsh environments, away from home in a strange country, quickly reinforced how blessed I have been by the special people in my life. From rewriting my will to painful goodbyes, the journey had already begun.

The second part of this journey is about the daily physical and mental demands made on me and how to work with them.... I am glad that I am able to enrich the lives of others who are less fortunate than me. This strengthens my desire to succeed. To show children their unlimited potential is something I am passionate about. In doing this journey, I want to show children that whatever they set their minds to, they can achieve....

The environment here (in the Gobi desert) is dry, desolate and hot. Some areas remind me of the gnarled, rocky, barren Richtersveld, others resemble the semi-arid flatlands of the Karoo, while others are like the dune sea of the Kalahari Basin. The Great Wall in this region is made of compacted mud and is extremely eroded. We often find ourselves looking for the next fortress or look-out tower in order to get our bearings. Thank goodness for our Garmin GPS! The watchtowers were manned to warn of Mongol attacks. The signal systems were either by sound or smoke. If a large-scale invasion was imminent, smoke signals were sent from tower to tower until they reached Beijing!

Because of the heat, we run in the mornings and occasionally walk in the above-35 degree heat of the afternoon to avoid dehydration. Our tactic is to average 35 kilometres a day in week 1....

We have covered 230 kilometres in the first week. What a pleasure to have a rest day! It is critical that we rest once a week or we risk long-term injury. So far so good. One day at a time ... It's how we should live in reality, but seldom do!

Already I craved time alone, after spending most of my days with the same person, which I was not used to, even though he was my friend. I called Ben and Mandi. I analysed maps, checked equipment and sent e-mails. I guess a part of me was trying to establish that I wasn't totally isolated, in a foreign place with alien people, doing a pretty crazy thing: I needed to keep alive the umbilicus between me and my home and loved ones. And yet another part of me loved it here. That part was the explorer and adventurer, always pushing my boundaries, knowing from experience that coming out alive would make me feel more alive than I ever could by playing it safe and doing the things that other 'normal' people did day by day.

But the time by myself also made me realise that I am a social animal and, as such, sought the company of others. Sitting in my room in the cheap hotel, I wondered if I could find that balance. I got off my bed and went to David's room to chat.

'Let's just plan our week ahead, have the rest day as our goal, and then bite it off a day at a time,' I said, closing the door before heading to bed.

The terrain on the second week was pretty much like that on the first. But the way our bodies felt wasn't. David had started developing a blister on his right ankle. I started experiencing a familiar pain that really worried me. It was the same pain I had experienced when I did my Plett to Cape Town run at age 17. The same pain that had reoccurred in 1999 on my Wild Child run. That very same pain that got me to say 'never again' more than once before. The pain under the balls of my feet. By day three of the second week I was hurting inside of five kilometres each day.

'Shit! This can't be happening. Please, not now, not here, not so soon,' I literally screamed at the desert.

By week three a new pattern had emerged. You know you're going to hurt. Get to 30 kilometres. Get your shoes off. Lie back with your feet elevated and relax and breathe. Stuff the idea of getting to the rest day goal. Just hit 30 kilometres. Be pain-free for half an hour or so. Feel pain for another 15 kilometres. Break down the day: three-quarters, two-thirds, halfway, one-third.... It made sense but still felt dreadful. Rest day became the day to reassess and rekindle the big dream. I would ask myself a simple question towards the end of rest day: 'Can I do this for another week?' Always the answer would be 'yes'. It was relatively easy when I wasn't feeling the pain! At the end of each day I would lie in my tent in the dark: 'Can I do this again tomorrow?' I'd whisper to myself.

And so it was that on one rest day I redefined how I planned to get through the ordeal. I wrote it all down so it made sense and I could see it and reread it whenever courage flagged. I had been doing it in practice, but I wanted to internalise the logic and diarise what was happening.

I also needed to make my goal smaller, much smaller.

I would break the big dream down into bite-sized chunks: a world-first meant 'get to lunch time', then 'get to my tent', then 'can I do this tomorrow?' Then, at the end of a rest day, 'can I do this for another week?' As I read my notes again and again, I wrote next to each question, 'YES!' in large letters and, as I wrote, I said it out loud.

After scripting my plan on that rest day I rehearsed it every night in my tent. Lying alone, I would touch Benjamin's stone. 'Remember how much you have to be grateful for,' I would repeat, sometimes many times over.

I would thank my Maker (because I believe that life, all life, is not a chance happening; I believe everything is connected and that we are all born into greatness and to not live out our lives to our fullest potential is to abuse our Creator) and, after switching off my headlamp, I would ask myself the same question every single night like a mantra: 'Can I do this again tomorrow?' And always, as part of the ritual, the answer would be 'Yes'. I would say it quietly but with firm conviction in the desert darkness. 'Yes!' Like a Buddhist monk, it was the repetition of the mantra that was the magic formula for overcoming apparent physical constraints.

It's hard to keep your humour in situations like this, but now I can look back and laugh at the similarity between my plight then and the joke about how do you eat an elephant – one bite at a time. Somewhat less humour-ous, but no less ironic, is the famous quote from Chairman Mao's famous *Little Red Book*, coined during the Long March of the Chinese Communist forces in 1934: 'A journey of 1,000 miles starts with a single step.' In other words, just as I was doing, you get through adversity by taking it one little bit at a time.

13

Merciful Rest

REST DAY WAS A TIME OF RELAXATION, reflection, introspection and an opportunity to re-assess and confirm my commitment. It also presented David and me with time to relax together with the team and plan the next week ahead. I suggested that each rest day we have a team debriefing. During these meetings David and I would praise the positives, addressing each individual, and then suggest if anything could be improved upon. In this way no-one should be offended but rather incentivised and their importance to the team reinforced. I tried to explain how vital they all were to the success of the expedition.

Rest day was not just a day, but something more precious to look forward to and savour: it was a full 36 hours – in other words a night, the following day and a second night. I got to particularly love the last afternoon before rest day. With 10 or 15 kilometres left at the end of around a 250-kilometre week, the feeling was exhilarating. I felt stronger and a little more confident as the weeks went by and became a month. The pain under my feet hadn't dissipated at all, even though 'Doc' Michael regularly massaged them. Sometimes it was so bad the tendons under my arches felt like they would snap. But stopping meant instant relief. Lunch times were also a respite from the pain. Removing my shoes and socks, lying on my back and elevating my legs to about 70 degrees had become a treasured ritual.

David often did the same. The small blister on his right ankle had developed into a massive beast. We named it The Monster. We would often eat in this beautiful pain-free position. The evenings after running into camp were even more rewarding – wearing slops or barefoot, feet up in my tent; mercifully weightless legs. So the thought of rest day was like a 'forgetting' time. It became a sanctuary from pain and a celebration of achievement. It was an almost sacred space, where I could blow gently on the dying red coals of my soul and rekindle them. I could re-affirm my dream and, in doing so, add fresh fuel to the embers and let the fire of my heart burn bright again.

If we were near a decent-sized town or city, even if it was 50 kilometres away, we'd opt to drive there for the rest day and then drive back to our last GPS point to pick up the start point for the new week. It gave me the opportunity to enjoy the culture of the people of this remote tract of China, being amongst strangers from a strange culture. It also presented the possibility of a hot shower and a real bed. All the little things I'd normally take for granted now became big rewards.

On one rest day, in a small rural village, I wandered the dirt roads between the mud and stone dwellings. A huge, lumbering ox, with a heavy wooden yoke over his neck adding to his burden, pulled an ancient cart laden with bright yellow corn. I felt like I was walking in a bygone era, as though I was a space traveller in an alien world. I could not understand the language. I couldn't relate to the way of life around me. The village seemed to exist as a separate entity, lost in time and space, the villagers not aware of the world around them and, if any of them were, it probably didn't matter.

Most of the flat-roofed homes were adorned with layers of maize drying in the sun. On the corners of some homes were little metal contraptions resembling old coffee grinders. They were clamped or bolted onto the eaves. I watched a man, squatting precariously on the not-too-stable corner of his roof, pushing cob after cob into the mouth at the top of the grinder and turning the handle on the side. *Grrrr, grrrr, grrrr* moaned the grinder, as the kernels were milled to a coarse powder. The staple diet in the rural north-west is maize, a dry-land crop native to the arid regions of north-central America.

Piles of the powder would be laid out on a compacted bit of ground that was so smooth it looked as though it had been polished. Women wearing breathing masks and wielding long, forked sticks with nets woven from palm fronds or maize leaves, rhythmically tossed the powder into the air. The coarser material dropped close by, while the finer powder drifted slowly to one side in the near-windless conditions. I stood mesmerised by the slow, patient and time-old dance of the masked women winnowing the maize from the chaff.

The meat of choice in these parts is pork. Meandering through the zigzag lanes, I would see many pigs, some tied up in rough cages and others in sties dug into the hard ground. In some of the larger towns where motorbikes were prevalent, I saw live pigs – sometimes up to three – strapped onto the bikes – one on each side like panniers, the other on the back like a passenger. Donkeys, the most versatile and gentle of all beasts of burden, often hauled loads so big the animal was dwarfed under them. They were also regularly slaughtered and eaten.

Running into one village to rendezvous with the team for a rest day, we heard a spine-chilling bellowing ahead of us.

'What the hell is that?' gasped David.

'Geez, sounds like some animal in trouble,' I panted back.

We slowed to a walk as the sound continued, getting closer.

'It's coming from in there,' said David, pointing to the typical red-tiled square entrance of a home.

When we came alongside the entrance we could see a donkey foal tethered a few metres from its mother. The mother was lying on her side, her front and hind legs bound. Her throat was being sawed – not cut, sawed with an old hacksaw. All the while both foal and mom bellowed their fear and pain to each other and the world. My natural instinct was to fly into the bunch of assholes standing around laughing and kick the crap out of them. I could honestly have killed them and I would have felt little remorse. I could have rationalised that this was just how they did things there, and to them those animals were just food, like plastic-wrapped meat in a supermarket is to us. But instead I was gripped by a similar feeling to one I had felt when catching poachers many years before. I was horrified and disgusted by what I saw. I felt ashamed at the cruelty of humanity. Thank goodness for my good friend. Sensing my anger, David grabbed my arm firmly.

'Don't,' he said, pulling me past the open doorway. 'We're the strangers here, we can't interfere, it won't make any difference except maybe wreck our journey,' he said calmly. He was right, of course, but my anger was real and I wanted to save the poor beast.

'At least kill the thing decently,' I said loudly to no-one in particular. I wanted to saw someone's head off slowly, thinking that would teach them a lesson but knowing it wouldn't; though it did help me to vent my anger and hatred a little. I was to see a lot more cruelty on this journey, but it never got any easier. While I am not against killing an animal for food – in fact, later, the success of the expedition depended on us getting meat and fat to eat – I am vehemently opposed to cruelty in any shape or form. When we lose respect for the very things that provide us with support and food, we lose respect for other creatures and then for ourselves.

■ THE RECCE TRIP IN 2005 FROM TOP DOWN:
The old Beijing train station.
The ornate lock on my door at William's farmhouse.
Great Wall mural at Beijing airport.
Our first steps in search of the Great Wall.

■ **ABOVE:** Seeing the Wall for the first time, through dense bush. The trees would be lifeless when we returned here in winter more than a year later. It was still some two kilometres away.
LEFT AND BELOW: Logistical planning in South Africa.
BELOW LEFT: William showing us the picture of the same tower in the Gobi he'd taken some 20 years earlier.

■ **OPPOSITE:** Meeting the elusive William Lindesay was a definitive moment, for without him, I'm not certain whether this journey would have come to fruition. Being on the Wall for the first time was an extremely emotional moment. I did 25 kilometres barefoot to really get to feel what I was going to be in for a year later. William called me the white bushman.

■ **ABOVE:** The team: Lee, Little Chang, Changa, Lunga, myself, David, Piou, Michael (Doc), Lilly and Hans (in front).

■ **ABOVE:** The support crew also had to navigate some serious terrain at times.
LEFT: I saw many human bones that were exposed over years of relentless dust storms. In these desolate areas there was no-one to rebury the long-forgotten Wall builders.
BELOW: The desert reclaims the Wall.

■ **TOP:** Deforestation and unsuitable farming practices have cut deep scars through the landscape, causing massive erosion.
ABOVE: Ancient Chinese architecture evokes a sense of a bygone era.

■ **THIS PAGE:** I saw very little regard for nature – environmental destruction, pollution and cruelty to animals were common sights.

The first time I ate donkey meat I had no idea what it was. Shaved, ham-like pieces of the flesh were rolled, dipped in oil, seasoned with spices and chilli, mixed with boiled vegetables and eaten hot. It was actually really good. Pig-intestine stew, on the other hand, was not. This was also boiled, in large clay pots with a hole in the base for a fire. Occasionally, the head of the pig would bubble away for good measure. Lilly told me it would make me extra strong! I would eat the stew quickly, holding my breath and with my eyes closed. The bubbling broth really stank. I learned early on in the journey to eat whatever I could get.

'Eat as much as you can,' Shelly told me on the phone from South Africa. 'If you can't get the right nutrients, eat whatever is available,' she'd insisted.

In the high mountains, with temperatures well below freezing, we could not risk our immune systems packing up. By that stage we had already lost a good five kilos each and there was still a long way to go. Extreme weight loss could end in death as a result of our bodies not being able to recover the harsh running regimen we were imposing on them. That had been the ultimate fate of Captain Robert Falcon Scott and his ill-fated South Pole team: it has been calculated they would have needed around 6,500 calories a day, but were getting only about 5,000. They had slowly starved to death, the situation made worse by compromised immune systems – not to mention the crippling cold.

A strange phenomenon in these really remote villages was the communication system with party officials in the cities: primitive village conditions contrasted with a mobile-phone tower standing out like a metal monolith, stark and alien. Often a big blue and white sign, in Mandarin and English, with the words 'China Mobile', would let the people know who supplied the communications. Party officials would send propaganda messages via bulk SMS. Even more alien than the tower sentinels were the satellite dishes on many of the roofs, big white saucers standing out in stark contrast to the tan-coloured mud buildings.

A common sight on the gravel streets were shallow, mirrored wok-like discs a little larger than a TV satellite dish. A metal rod protruded from the top edge, with an elbow bend and a hook. Hanging from the hook would be a kettle being fired to boiling point by solar energy. Thankfully, the donkey incident was not an everyday occurrence and the contrasts and colours in the villages, the friendliness of the people and their humble generosity, more often than not lifted my spirit.

The average house had a shiny, tiled façade indicating the entrance. The tiles were usually bright red with a mosaic of bamboo stems and birds or some tranquil water scene. This was odd, because in reality there was nothing like it around for perhaps a thousand kilometres. Maybe it was an attempt to bring the beauty of the lush green of southern China into the arid north. The entrance led into a courtyard, which could house pigs, a donkey or two, or maybe an old, dilapidated tractor. The rectangular home was at the far end of the yard. The entire property would be surrounded by four walls, with the windows of the house always looking inwards to the courtyard.

On that particular day, as David and I explored the village together, an old man appeared in his doorway and stared at the apparition approaching. As we drew nearer, his wizened, wrinkled face cracked into a broad smile, exposing a mouth full of broken, stained teeth. Many silver fillings sparkled in the harsh desert sun. Under a tattered straw hat, round goggle-like glasses covered a quarter of his face. One hand held the remnants of a rolled cigarette and the other an old plaited goat-skin whip. I noticed his whip hand had only two fingers and a thumb. The knobbled, calloused knuckles where his fingers used to be had healed badly into large, probably painful, arthritic bumps.

He beckoned to us with much animation, to follow him. We smiled and obliged.

'Nǐ hǎo' (pronounced 'nee how'), I said, bowing my head in the traditional Chinese fashion.

'Nǐ hǎo' (greetings), he nodded.

Sitting on wooden blocks, David and I entertained him and his family with our presence. They had likely never left their village nor ever seen a foreigner, let alone one from Nam Fey (South Africa). They sliced sweet melon and generously shared it with us. They chattered loudly and laughed among themselves. I laughed at their laughter and marvelled at their simple existence. They lived off the desert, taking anything they could, to survive to the next season.

Rest days were also a time for reflection on the week past. A time for e-mailing family and friends and for writing blogs for the website and sending pictures. They were never long enough. Always too soon it was time to move on.

14

Scorched Earth

LONG, ROCKY, HILLY DAYS SAW US NAVIGATE from tower to distant tower through an eerie, arid landscape. Deserted, ruined old villages of broken, heaped stone and clay paid tribute to our most precious and priceless commodity – water. As the wells had run dry, the people had been forced to leave these barren hills in the hope of eking out a living elsewhere. A week would pass by and I would not see a single soul. This was an uninhabitable, inhospitable land.

But clearly it had not always been so. North and north-west China has a highly variable and erratic rainfall. This is coupled with regular occurrences of high winds and droughts, which make the area susceptible to dust storms and severe soil erosion. Before the arrival of the first pastoralists, however, the landscape existed in a delicate state of balance. The native plants growing here were adapted to deal with the erratic changes in water availability and created their own microclimate. Forest trees and shrubs would shade and shelter smaller grasses growing below, and increase the availability of water. A healthy ecosystem acts like a sponge, retaining water and increasing soil and atmospheric humidity, thereby enabling the growth of many more sensitive species. They also provide a habitat for animals and micro-organisms, which in turn break down nutrients and return them in available forms back to the plants' roots, as well as assisting with seed dispersal and germination. They thus ensure the longevity and renewal of the plant community.

Unfortunately, as soon as humans arrived several thousand years ago they started clearing natural vegetation to make space for crops, and hunted wildlife. In this way, they made the remaining cover more exposed to environmental stresses and initiated an irreversible spiral towards death and desolation. Remaining pockets were now more susceptible to damage by storms, drought and overgrazing by the increasing numbers of livestock and started degrading. As soon as ground was cleared for agriculture and ploughed regularly, the originally fertile soil, permeated by a living network of roots and insects, lay bare baking in the harsh sun and turned into sterile sand. It has since been eroded away by rain and wind and leaves nothing but a dead lunar landscape, where nothing will be able to grow in the next couple of millennia. The only plants I could see now were the occasional scrub-like bushes scattered every 10 metres or so. They were no higher than 30 centimetres and did not have the option of moving on like the humans did. They simply survived or died. Most had died, as was evidenced by the brittle skeletons of tinder that bore testament to their existence.

With their own forests long gone, China is now following in the footsteps of other more 'developed' countries, such as the USA and Europe, that have to exploit other countries' natural resources after exhausting their own. China is now one of the two leading importers of timber from tropical rainforests in countries like the Philippines and Indonesia, repeating the process of exploitation and subsequent ecological death all over again, until there is nothing left.

Forests were even destroyed to build the Wall. In order to move the large, chiselled rocks from the valleys to the high, knife-edged mountain ridges above, forests were cleared for scaffolding, for pulley systems to be constructed and continuous fires used to boil rice to make cement, as well as charcoal fires for the kilns in which the endless supply of bricks were baked. The huge cauldrons of rice porridge and limestone gruel were hauled up the steep slopes to cement the millions of bricks used to build the Wall. Trees were cut to build villages, to warm homes during the freezing winters and to cook food for the millions of workers and soldiers.

Some of the valleys and hills that are barren, dead desert today, were once forested landscapes, or savanna and grasslands. Then again, so was much of north Africa when the Romans first got there. We passed many sections of mud Wall where wooden poles protruded from the eroded sides. Wall builders used whatever materials were available in any area and the poles had been placed as reinforcing between layers of mud. The task was to build an impressive defence system across China's northern frontier, certainly not to worry about the future of the forests.

There is a story of why so few birds remain in certain areas of the great north-west. Thousands upon thousands of birds would be attracted by the seed sown to feed the vast army of Wall labourers. The birds would eat much of the seeds and so, to save the food, and hence the people, a general had ordered hundreds of thousands of long poles to be cut and sharpened. The troops patrolled the fields, holding the poles above them, poking at the birds when they attempted to land. Because the birds could not land to eat they literally died of exhaustion and hunger. This story is often used to illustrate the might of a united China.

I remembered how I had seen so many birds in the arid Kalahari savanna of Botswana, but here in the otherwise similar Gobi, apart from the occasional owl living in the wall or a lone kestrel sweeping low in search of prey, there was nothing. Of course the Kalahari has only the sparsest of human settlement, whereas China has the world's largest population: a staggering 1.3 billion people, or one-fifth of the Earth's total!

After more than 600 kilometres of barren ups and downs on brittle gravel, the hills levelled to gently rolling, sandy hills and ancient, dry flood plains. Although it was barely perceptible, we were moving gradually upwards as the days wore on. With the increase in altitude came colder nights. In the distance, I noticed a dark grey cloud lying low on the horizon. As the day wore on, the cloud, now looking almost black, seemed much bigger than I had at first thought.

There were no reference points in the desolation, such as a building or a windmill, to put a scale to things. What looked like a distant little lump of a hill at first, would become much bigger than I had thought as we neared it. The dark cloud, lying like a heavy crumpled blanket, appeared to be incubating a giant black egg that shimmered, distorted in the mirage's obscurity.

I felt like I was walking slap into a post-apocalyptic science-fiction movie scene: loud clanging, reverberating, pulsing machinery, rusty grinding trucks moving like ants to and from the epicentre. Then it hit me: it was a giant old coal-fired power station. Massive metal ribs from some decaying mechanical carcass seemed to plead in desperation for the sun to relent. Here, where I thought no human life could possibly exist, where fragile nature should have been left free from the ravages of humankind, they had found one of nature's precious resources and were leaving their thanks with huge clouds of black soot.

'Will we take everything and leave only destruction and pollution behind us?' I asked myself.

China is the world's biggest producer and consumer of coal, accounting for over a quarter of the Earth's total. Three-quarters of China's energy consumption currently depends on coal. This is the main cause of its horrific air pollution and acid rain. I remembered in Beijing seeing many people wearing white face masks to protect them from the almost permanent cloud of yellow-grey smog that covers the city. But the country's reliance on coal has another, even more serious consequence in spin-off industries. It requires vastly more water to produce things like fertiliser and textiles from coal than from oil, which is how most other countries do it. One of China's greatest problems today is its scarcity of not just clean drinking water, but water generally.

The amazing growth of China's cities from 1953 to the present is staggering. In less than 50 years the number of large cities quintupled, to around 700. The old cities have also grown massively over the same period. As I ran across the vast openness of the desert, it all felt sterile. I wondered if these areas would, or could, ever become inhabited again. I thought of China's largest mega-project ever, the Great Wall, and it scared me to think just what the Chinese can achieve when they set their collective mind to the task.

The plan is to develop the remote north-west where there is already a severe water shortage. This solution is to move vast quantities of water from the wetter south of the country to the desert. Already, around 75 per cent of all China's lakes and most of its coastal seas are severely polluted. Most of the water needed for the growth of cities and agriculture comes from fossil water, or ancient water stored in huge underground aquifers. These aquifers are running dry and aren't going to be refilled any time soon.

China has two of the five longest rivers in the world, the Yangtze and the Yellow. They are being pumped out to irrigate lands to such an extent that the Yellow River, which we would see in a few weeks' time, now has only an erratic flow and in some years it no longer reaches the sea. In 1988 the Yellow River stopped flowing for 10 days. In 1997 the river stopped for a shocking 230 days!

And now the mighty Yangtze River is experiencing similar problems.

Yet China has embarked on a river-damming project so ambitious that it's frightening. The largest water impoundment in the world, the Three Gorges Dam project on the Yangtze River, is already almost complete. It will not only displace tens of thousands of people and inundate complex riverine ecosystems, but it will also impede the flow of the world's third-largest river. But how else can you sustain the world's biggest population? There is no easy answer. Also, the project to divert water to the north-west, the world's largest ever water-diversion project, is well underway. It should be on line by 2050 and cost around US$59-billion. But, in my view (as well as that of many other concerned people), the environmental damage will be 'priceless' and irreversible.

As I ran past the huge coal-fired metal monstrosity, coughing out its contaminating waste into the otherwise pristine desert air, I thought about why they wanted to move so much water out here. Western China, incorporating the desert I was running through, makes up more than half the country's land area. The Chinese government views the region as the key to national development and the only vital ingredient needed is water. Where there is water, there will be life. I had my answer.

It is a well-understood phenomenon that when you seriously mess with nature and cause wide-scale environmental degradation, we all ultimately suffer. This is well documented by the collapses of past civilisations, including the Maya, Khmer, the Polynesian inhabitants of Easter Island, the Anasazi of south-central America, even the once-mighty Roman Empire, when they disrupted water systems in order to grow their population beyond what an area can sustain naturally. These lessons are evident for all to see, yet we ignore them and blunder forward in the name of progress and economic growth – not to mention the mostly unchecked population growth of Third World nations.

These problems are by no means unique to China. It was just that being there brought it rather blatantly to my attention. Indeed, similar problems are facing many countries the world over. We are all connected in this little village of ours. Australia, which we see as being a thoroughly modern, successful and even progressive country, is currently also facing some of the worst water shortages and salinisation of vast tracts of its best agricultural lands. Large-scale dam and irrigation developments along the entire length of its largest river system, the Murray-Darling, have, much like in China, caused the rivers to frequently dry up before reaching the ocean in South Australia.

And South Africa is not exempt. We often look at the problems in other countries and ignore what is happening in our own backyard. Africa is historically a dry continent – and, with increased warming, becoming even drier. If a miracle happened and all global carbon emissions stopped tomorrow, it would still take decades for the momentum to slow and at least 50 years for the planet to regulate itself. So, what does that mean for Africa, and for me? Africa, already dealing with serious water shortages, will lose between 10 and 30 per cent of its current pool of fresh water over the next 10 years.

Although I knew a lot of these facts before going to China, running in the Gobi desert provided me with space and time to reflect on these things and then look more deeply into them when I returned home afterwards. The vastness of the land and the silence it provided created a space for introspection. While movies like Al Gore's *An Inconvenient Truth* and Leonardo Di Caprio's *The 11th Hour* had both done much to bring the plight of the planet – and what would happen to us if we didn't fix things quickly – to the attention of the general population, because they did not present enough practical solutions to you and me, I believe most people felt powerless to do anything to repair the problem.

When that happens, we feel emotionally impotent, we intellectually deny the truth and fall back into the blinkered rut of day-to-day existence. Hiding in the shallow logic of 'it isn't really happening' and 'it's not really my fault, or my problem to solve' becomes one giant conspiracy against the planet we rely on totally for our wellbeing. That, conveniently, allows us to go on with business as usual.

For me, China brought home just how serious the problem is. I wasn't just reading stuff in books, I was seeing it all around me. It provided a platform to look for real solutions in my life and created an opportunity for me to contribute, in whatever way I could, to saving this planet that has been dubbed 'spaceship Earth'. The image of Earth as a spaceship, travelling alone through a lonely universe, is used to show people how vulnerable we are: if we screw up things on this spaceship, hurtling as it is through the cosmos, there's nowhere else to go – we're toast.

I have a cabin at my special place in the Cape mountains called Beaverlac where I do bush camps for children. When trying to explain the 'finite planet' to them, I often use a simple analogy of a pet hamster.

'You have your pretty pet hamster in its cage,' I say. 'It has all of its basic needs met – water, food and shelter. It eats seeds and even stores them when it has too many, in case you forget to feed it tomorrow,' I continue. 'But, poor thing, it's lonely. So, we get him a wife. Because she now feels comfortable and safe, she has babies. The babies grow quickly and they have babies. There are no predators to eat the hamsters, like there would be in nature,' I explain. 'So, as long as you keep giving them food and water, they keep breeding.'

Then, eventually, something changes. The strongest hamsters start to kill and even eat the weak ones – usually the newest babies. The children, now horrified, usually ask 'why?' at this point! 'Because of the stress of too many hamsters in one place,' I tell them, 'they start fighting. This causes more stress which results in death. The cage is finite in size, it can't get any bigger. It can hold only so many hamsters comfortably. Of course, if you want to, you can just ask your mom to go out and buy another cage,' I say half in jest. 'Now imagine the Earth is like that cage. It can hold only so many people before we start to behave just like the hamsters. The only difference – and it's a big difference – is that we can't go out and buy another Earth,' I emphasise. 'We have to live within the limits of what the Earth can provide, and there are very definite limits.'

The amazing thing for me is that when I explain this to children, they get it, they understand. It's the adults who usually go into denial with a barrage of arguments – and all those arguments achieve is to reveal the short-sighted self-interest of people who justify why they don't want to change!

Feeling the hot sun on my deeply tanned skin, I thought of Beaverlac, with its abundance of water all year round. I thought of the zipline *foefie* slide I rig up over the camp's main rock pool in the middle of summer and the joy on the kids' faces as they fly through the air and plunge into the deep, pure mountain pool. My water bladder was near empty and the small sips I rationed myself were warm. We saw some maize fields ahead. 'Irrigation,' I thought.

'We should find water there,' David jerked me out of my daydream. We followed the edge of the corn field until we came across a narrow irrigation ditch that formed one branch of an intricate part of a rotational crop irrigation system. We stripped off and washed ourselves in the cool water. As I cupped the pure clear water that was pumped up from way below the surface to my mouth, I realised just how precious this was. I thought of how limited a resource it actually is and how, until it's not readily available, we take it for granted.

There are currently around six and a half billion people alive, on a planet that it has been calculated can comfortably sustain just four billion. It is a conservatively estimated fact that by 2050 there'll be around nine billion people on Earth: we don't need to be rocket scientists to realise we are facing a serious, potentially catastrophic situation. Unless we accept that we live on a finite Earth, with a certain carrying capacity, and that she needs to be protected *at all costs*, we will not survive as a species much longer. 'At all costs' means immediately, right now, today. We have to urgently address resource use and population growth. Paradoxically, China leads the way in showing the world what can be done to regulate population growth.

China's population is the largest in the world and was also the fastest growing, with a 5.4 per cent growth rate a year. In the 1980s the government realised the country wouldn't be able to support such an exponential birth rate. It instituted mandatory fertility control and by 2001 the growth rate was down to 1.3 per cent. When China initiated its population control policy, it was unique, but it has also been roundly criticised supposedly on humanitarian grounds. Iran has recently followed suit. The question is: while many countries recoiled in horror at China's solution, what are they going to do before they find themselves driven to seek even worse solutions to their population issues?

Rwanda's recent genocide comes to mind. People killed each other because land, water and food literally ran out. The results of overpopulation are real and affect us all. No country will be safe just because it believes itself to be sovereign and stable. People will go to where there is food and water. It's that simple. South Africa has a birth rate that is extremely high by the standards of most politically and economically stable countries, at around 2.6 per cent. We also have very limited water resources: what are we going to do about it here?

Our collective world legal system has been quick and right to punish acts that have resulted in the mass destruction of human life, such as the genocides of the World War Two Holocaust, that of the Pol Pot regime in Cambodia, in Rwanda, in the old Yugoslavia (Serbia) and possibly now in Sudan as well. We hold these people, and even whole nations, accountable for grievous crimes against humanity. Yet, there is no collective will or system in place holding societies accountable for what I believe to be *the* most grievous crime against humanity: namely destroying the world we will be leaving to our children and our grandchildren. Indeed, the environmental crimes we are perpetrating are the greatest crimes of all, because human populations always seem to bounce back after even the worst atrocities, but the Earth cannot heal faster than we are now injuring it.

Kyoto accords and the recent Copenhagen agreements are rendered impotent when the big nations like the USA and China put short-term national economic interests before global environmental ones. I truly believe that the December 2009 summit in Copenhagen was possibly one of the most important meetings, if not *the* most important, in the history of our species. While certain countries like the USA, China, India and South Africa agreed to certain important issues, nothing is legally binding and, therefore, no delivery is guaranteed. I see this as nothing short of the potential mass destruction of not millions, but billions of humans over the next few decades.

'Perhaps,' I say sadly to myself, 'this is nature's way of sorting out the problem.' After all, we have had ample opportunity.

In the past century we have destroyed so much natural habitat that the Earth is currently undergoing the greatest mass extinction of all time, not even closely equalled by the extinction of the dinosaurs around 65 million years ago. Between 25,000 and 35,000 species are going extinct every year. Most of the large, non-domesticated mammals we see today will not survive to 2050. That means, a child born today will be showing his or her children pictures of polar bears, cheetahs, rhinos, wild dogs, even lions, in books or zoos if they are that lucky. And what will he or she say: 'Sorry kids, we killed them all'?

It's hard to believe, I know, but the facts are there for anyone to see ... for anyone who *will* see. In our short-sightedness, driven by material greed and denial, we are destroying the rights of our children to a sustainable future. We are taking away their future happiness and leaving them only suffering. Isn't this the ultimate crime against humanity?

Leaving our irrigation-channel oasis, we plodded on, back into the dry desert nothingness ahead. With all my thoughts, fears and hopes somersaulting around in my head, I felt dizzy, as though in a waking nightmare. I looked at the bereft terrain around me and couldn't help wondering if I was staring at a scene of the whole Earth of the future.

15

Living Hell

ALTHOUGH IT WAS PAST MID-AUTUMN in the Gobi desert and the nights were getting colder, the days were still hot, with temperatures around the mid 30s. Our hottest day was 41 °C.

On one of those hot days we had just finished lunch and were enjoying legs-up with some of the support team, when a light but dry desert wind began to blow. Hans and Michael had gone on ahead to find a suitable camp spot for the night. We hadn't gone far into the afternoon's run when I received their GPS co-ordinates and saw we had only a gently undulating 12 kilometres or so to get there.

'Hey David, camp is only around 12 kays ahead,' I relayed.

GPS co-ordinates are 'as the crow flies', so the distance is always relative to the path you have to take on the ground. The maps we were using were A4 sheets photocopied from Chinese ones; so not only couldn't we read off much useful info, they were also highly inaccurate. I had tried to get hold of 1:50,000 maps, with contour intervals 20 metres apart – the kind we use for adventure racing back home – but it seemed they were unheard of in China.

'Only the military will have those,' William told us.

Our measly A4 copies were totally inconsistent. One section would be in 1:100,000 scale and the next page would be 1:500,000. On top of that, some of them had no contour lines at all. That meant there could be a huge eroded chasm five kilometres ahead and we would have no idea until we got there. We tended to base our day's plan on the general lay of the land and, overall – at that early stage at any rate – the terrain looked relatively runable.

At lunch we had opted to travel light, but that turned out to be a big mistake. Running in vests and shorts, we strapped on light waist belts: mine held 1.8 litres of water, a health bar, my small camera and cell phone. By travelling that light we aimed to kill the afternoon leg in about an hour and a bit. The warm wind was behind us as we headed off towards our GPS rendezvous point and the end of another hot, dry desert day.

I was running smoothly and felt good. My mind was freewheeling along and holding onto nothing in particular, when the song I had been desperately trying to shake out of my thoughts for the past few days returned: '*I've been through the desert on a horse with no name, It felt good to be out of the rain ...*' I had enjoyed it at first, but now it was really irritating me. Like a stuck record, it just went on and on: '*In the desert you can remember your name, 'Cause there ain't no-one for to give you no pain, na na naaa na, na na naaa na....*'

At first it had seemed really appropriate: '*After two days in the desert sun ...,*' but then '*After three days in the desert sun,*' it just wasn't so funny, or appropriate, anymore. It made me think of that disaster climbing movie *Touching the Void* where Joe Simpson, with his one leg shattered and on the verge of death after days on the mountain and in the bowels of the glacier, gets stuck on that banal Boney M song '*Brown Girl in the Ring, na na na na naa*'. He refuses to die with such an awful song playing in loop mode in his head and, with his last ounce of life, he drags his weighted body like an anchor behind his arms, smack into the team's base camp latrine site. That filthy stench had guided him home.

'Geez, I wish I could lose this stupid song,' I said to David.

'What song?' he said, glancing at me.

Then it happened.

We had covered about five kilometres when I heard what sounded like dynamite exploding somewhere behind us. We had been told there wouldn't be any sand storms this time of year and so were ill-prepared for what we saw brewing. It was still a clear blue-sky day but the warm tail wind suddenly got a whole lot hotter and much stronger. It felt as though we were in a wind tunnel that was also an oven. It was really hot. I slowed down and looked back: a dark, thick bank of orange-brown turmoil was tumbling along the horizon toward us like a scene from the Apocalypse. I stopped in disbelief and called to David, who was now some way ahead of me.

He turned around.

'Hell,' he exclaimed.

It was an accurate description of the scene, and the fate that awaited us. The boiling mass of dust cloud was scary enough, but it was the sheer speed of the monster chasing us that caused the panic.

'We're going to have to run for our lives,' I screamed to David through the howling gusts of hot wind.

The Great Wall in this part of the Gobi was little more than a two-metre-high heap of sand, looking as though a giant mole had trundled along just below the ground for a few hundred kilometres … or maybe a giant sand worm right out of the sci-fi *Dune* trilogy! It looked like this because the mud structure had been pounded by dust storms for 500 years. There were no large rocks lying around or buttresses behind which to shelter. There seemed to be no escape. Our support crew would not be able to reach us in time. We ran for our lives as the hot tsunami of dust lapped at our heels. In my terrified state I kept telling myself to stay calm. I knew that my chances of survival would be better if I could stop myself from panicking. But I wasn't calm; can you remain calm when a forest fire is about to catch you? David slowed down and took out the camera and took a few shots. 'Has he gone nuts?' I thought to myself.

'Run,' I screamed at him, 'just run.'

He didn't need much encouragement and was off like a scrub hare. Within 10 minutes I couldn't see him and yet he was no more than four metres ahead of me. The noise of the wind, the thunder cracking around me, the sun a pale yellow disc being eaten by the pumpkin-coloured giant.

'So is this how it's going to end,' I thought in my choking fear.

'Hug the Wall,' I shouted to David, hidden somewhere in the frightening swirl. 'Stay close to the Wall. Follow the Wall!'

I had removed my vest and was trying to use it as a mask to block the dust entering my lungs. My eyes were weeping gritty tears, which made it difficult to see. I began coughing and spitting to expel the dough-like paste that was making me gag. At one point I had to stop to vomit. As I continued, the dust, about the consistency of cement powder, caked my mouth and nose and caused me to gag again. Because I was running so hard, I was also breathing hard and fast. I thought maybe I should slow down so that I could breathe slower.

'We can't out-run this thing,' I thought, 'it's all around us, it's eating us up,' and then I thought of Benjamin and I didn't want to die, not now and certainly not like this.

And then a not-so-small miracle appeared: a single cubbyhole in the Wall, just big enough to hide the two of us in its cramped interior. We had not seen one of these for a few days. I guessed in times past nomadic shepherds must have scraped them out for just such emergencies. We scurried into the bur-row like petrified rabbits. Using our vests, we tried to block the entrance as best we could in a futile attempt to keep out the dust. We realised the worst was not over, not by a long shot, but that we were at least buying ourselves some time.

Sitting in a desperate inner silence – the rolling thunder playing bass to the howling wind outside – I missed Benjamin more than ever. What had I done; why had I risked my life like this; how could I have done this to him?

The many thoughts rolled uncontrolled around in my head like tumbleweeds. I thought about the 16 scientists who had died in just such a sand storm the year before we'd done our recce trip: anxious people struggling to breathe, watching their friends dying around them, knowing they would follow soon, choking on the paste as it allowed one last desperate gasp at life. The terror consumed me. David stuck his finger down his throat and vomited. I followed suit.

After what seemed an eternity, but was probably no more than an hour, the wind and dust howled past us like an express train and faded just as rapidly as it had approached. A few token drops of rain fell as we crept from our hole like two timid animals. Both of us had wet streaks down our cheeks. Whether from watering eyes or desperate tears I wasn't sure, I just knew how grateful I was to be alive. We walked in silence, those last few kilometres to camp. I watched the vast rolling wave from which we had been delivered boiling off into the distant nothingness of time and space. I wept silently at the joy of being alive and I felt very humbled.

Looking back, I had been incredibly present, similar to when you are sitting in your car, drifting slowly towards the rear end of the car in front of you, but your brakes are engaged and there is nothing you can do to slow the momentum. In these moments time seems stretched, every second lasting an eternity, making you painfully aware of your utter incapacity to change the outcome of what will happen next. Seemingly insignificant details burn themselves into your consciousness and refuse to leave your traumatised mind for a long time afterwards. I can still conjure the taste of the cement powder-like dust in my mouth, its dry stickiness filling my mouth and throat; the smell of chalk in my nostrils; my body prickling with goosebumps in spite of the heat. I have never felt so vulnerable and afraid, nor wanted to live so badly. It's like your brain function speeds up exponentially and thoughts and feelings flood through you uncontrollably. A few seconds turn into a long, tortuous spell in which to ponder decisions you have made in your life, to regret and to wonder 'what if?'

In the days that followed I became very introspective. I questioned my existence, my uniqueness and my self-imposed loneliness – or rather, I should say aloneness. I thought of us as a species and how we came to be where we are today in the great evolution of things. I appreciated the gift of my life immensely and vowed that I would live the rest of it to the fullest.

We are the only mammals blessed with a unique and special gift. Chimpanzees don't have it; elephants don't have it; dolphins don't have it, only we do. In the front of our brains lies the frontal lobe that allows us do something extraordinary: we can be in the present, reflect on the past, learn from it and use that knowledge to shape our future. There is great power in that, but it is an unfortunate thing that so few people acknowledge this gift, or use it wisely. All too often we need a crisis in our lives – like staring death in the face – before we can muster the courage to embrace change as a necessary part of our growth. In the Mandarin dialect the word 'crisis' is made up of two symbols: *cri*, meaning fear or danger, and *sis*, meaning opportunity. So it is between success and failure: people who see the danger and allow themselves to become victims to fear are doomed to failure. But those who see the opportunity in the danger will usually rise above it and move toward a fuller, more successful existence.

During the course of our lives at some stage we all become victims of fear. Some people are perpetual worriers. Yet very little of what we worry about ever materialises. Was it Franklin D Roosevelt who said, 'we have nothing to fear but fear itself'? We spend vast amounts of energy worrying 'what if this or that happens; what will people think of me if....' Much of human behaviour is fear motivated.

There are people who go to work not because they like it or are good at it, but because they have to, because of the fear of poverty, or loss of status. They earn a salary to afford a few days a month being happy. If they could just stop worrying about their problems. They are not following their passion, or allowing any kind of passion or love into their lives, but are rather submitting to their fears. Eventually the fear wins and they turn to some kind of numbing escape such as alcohol, gambling or drugs that ultimately leaves them empty, spent and disillusioned.

If you let fear in, its roots grow really fast, anchoring around your heart and slowly suffocating your spirit. In extreme cases, ordinary stresses of life manifest themselves in diseases like depression, cancer, heart attacks and strokes. But for most people caught in the daily grind of life, it leads to a sense of emptiness – a mid-life crisis, the sense of a life not spent but wasted. Maybe this is the 'originl sin' that will trip us up for not following our hearts and leading full and happy lives.

I once heard a wonderful definition of Hell: arriving at the end of your life and meeting the person you could have been. Apart from fear there are other forms of motivation: one is material or incentive motivation, and the other is psychological or attitude motivation. When an employer offers an employee a reward like a bonus or promotion, they'll tend to work with more passion and drive. But incentive also means someone else is controlling their life. Incentives keep having to get bigger to maintain the motivation: the novelty of the new car or new house wears off in time and we find ourselves chasing the next 'big fix'.

Attitude motivation is internal and gives us total control over our lives: it is powerful beyond measure.

There is a wonderful story of a small boy who fully understood attitude motivation: One day, standing in his yard, he held a cricket bat in one hand and a ball in the other.

He was talking out loud to himself as kids often do: 'I'm the best batsman in my school,' he declared as he tossed the ball into the air. *Swish* went the bat, *plunk* went the ball as it hit the ground. Pausing, but undeterred, he picked it up and tried again: 'the best in the province,' he said, more confidently. He missed again. He looked first at the bat then at the ball. Throwing it higher, he shouted: 'I'm the best batsman in the world.' Again, *plunk* went the ball. He looked at the ball on the ground at his feet. Shaking his head, he said 'Heck, I'm the greatest bowler in the world!'

And so it is, that if you believe it you can honestly choose what you want to be. But choose carefully, with your intuition, and have the courage to trust your choice! It is vital that we allow ourselves the privilege of quiet space, for it is there we discover the passion that drives us to our heart's desire, to our destiny. China gave me that opportunity and I embraced it. It provided space for me to be alone with myself and my thoughts for an unusually long time: not many adults get to use that kind of time for personal growth. How I used that time, and who and what I invited into that space, was up to me. I could go through a whole day and just absorb feelings. I wanted to and often lusted for it. It made me feel vital, even when my being was engulfed in physical pain. The pain, the loneliness, the introspection made me feel supernaturally alive – and I craved it.

Religious mystics and people who have experimented with LSD speak of how they have felt close to the spirit of nature, and close to their god. Often during this period of 'the great run', whether I was out on the desert plains consumed by the pain in my feet, or hearing the howl of the wind at night shaking my tent as I tried to sleep, I always, without exception, felt a deep connectedness to the Earth and experienced a spiritual sense of being close to my own maker. You could call it my 'road to Damascus' moment, or my spiritual awakening; I felt it completely and I wanted more. You could say that I was born again out there in the Gobi desert, in the sense that my life would change profoundly and I would be left with a deep sense of purpose that would chart the course of the rest of my life.

I am a strong man, physically and mentally. I am determined enough to die in a physical fight if I have to fight for something I believe in. I am also headstrong enough to argue a point – even if it makes me unpopular, or makes me look like the fool in a group – if I believe in something strongly enough. I know I am driven, but what is this thing that drives me; what makes me run across my home province, or halfway across China? I know it is not just the need for an adventure. It is also not only to help poor young children smile – even though those are real enough motivations. I am driven to trying to save the world – one step at a time, you could say.

Do you think I'm crazy? Do you not feel, or have you never felt, the same? Ask yourself – especially if you have children: 'Who am I deep inside, and am I doing something worthwhile with my life? Will I be able to look back on a life well lived and well spent?' Running in the desert, feeling alone, I got pissed off with humanity and I got pissed off with myself for living a lie. I carried on running, escaping, running tired and often angry, punishing myself for my own sins against nature, as well as those of my fellow humans. The desert seemed to echo my emptiness and my pain. I desperately wanted my life to have a lasting purpose and so I ran on to find it.

16

Breaking the Pain Barrier

WE HAD BEEN RUNNING SINCE FIRST LIGHT from one broken, stony hilltop to the next. The Wall was so ruined here that running on it was treacherous. The bricks had collapsed into piles of loose rubble, as though they had been poured in an endless line by giant tipping trucks. We knew from the map that the small town of Jingtai was somewhere south of us and that the mighty Yellow River (Huang He) was somewhere ahead as we headed out of the realm of sand and into the broken rocky foothills of the Qilian Shan. But where? The harsh terrain showed no evidence of water. There was no greenery in sight. Then suddenly the earth opened up in front of us as we found ourselves standing on a high plateau, probably 1,000 metres above the Yellow River. Deciding whether to go down and follow the bank or to stay on the plateau and traverse above the valley, ended up being a long debate between David and me.

I reluctantly accepted David's view of going as straight down as we could. I judged from the size of the river and the steepness of the terrain that the meanders would run up against steep cliffs with no embankment to walk on. And that was indeed what transpired. We spent the best part of an hour carefully negotiating our way down into the hot valley. I led the way at a serious pace along the left bank of the river. Rounding a bend, I stared in total dismay at what lay in front of me: a smooth, sheer cliff ran vertically down into the fast-moving murky, muddy water. We had two options: go back or attempt to climb out at a point before the cliff became too precarious. Crossing the river would be potentially fatal, as the current was strong, the river was at least 100 metres wide and we couldn't see around the next meander. We couldn't see very far above us either, and therefore couldn't judge the terrain ahead, so we decided to climb out of the valley at that point – it turned out to be a bad call.

The slope was extremely steep and consisted of broken shale. Using our trekking poles was vital for bracing on the steep and crumbly incline. We were about 200 metres up the slope, with David scrambling up ahead of me, when he lost his footing and fell. He tumbled passed me and came to a stop on a ledge.

'Geez, you okay?' I shouted as I carefully moved down to him.

'I think I'm fine,' he replied. But when he tried to stand I knew something was wrong. He winced as he tried to put weight on his right leg.

The day had clouded over. There was an ominous grey blanket hanging low over the shattered, relentless landscape, as though it wanted to suffocate the Earth. David was struggling to walk and we had little idea of where we were going. I knew we were moving in more or less the right direction, as I had seen two Great Wall watchtowers high on the distant hills before we had begun our descent into the valley. There was no chance of communicating with the crew as there was no signal there. We had no Wall to follow, no idea where we were or the distance to the team. The day was nearing its gloomy end and we were moving over hectic terrain at a snail's pace. I calculated we were covering a kilometre every 30 minutes, and that was actual travel, not 'as the crow flies'. Then the rain started. Hard desert drops.

'What next?' I thought despondently.

So far we'd had only one day of light drizzle on the entire journey and now, in this fractious place, at the end of a long day, with David injured, it rained with intent. The ground became slippery, which slowed us down even more. Eventually, moving over the stony hills, I found a valley with a semblance of a track running along its base and snaking in the general direction of the river.

'There must be a track or road along the bank back there,' I shouted to David in the now-gusting evening.

'Just keep moving and I'll scout ahead,' I said as I ran down a slope.

I followed the track for about two kilometres to ensure its meandering route held the general direction, then went back for David. He was in serious discomfort. We put on our head lamps and, finally, after five slow kilometres, we hit the river. We had climbed out of the valley and then made a wide arc back down to the river. There was, very fortunately, a jeep track of sorts along the bank. Then we saw a light flashing – Lunga had seen our head lamps. 'Good old Lunga,' I sighed.

David was quiet, clearly in pain and obviously worried about his future on the expedition. We had covered only about 800 kilometres at this point and, thank goodness, the next day was a rest one. We drove all the way back to the city of Wuwei where we could get David's leg X-rayed. Luckily he had only torn a muscle so Doc Michael strapped him and iced him. I spoke to David about his misgivings.

Voicing my personal philosophy on these matters, I said: 'It's up to you, my friend. It's all in your head,' I emphasised. 'You hold onto the dream, this is one setback among many we've had, and will still have, that's all.'

We had made a pact that if either of us was injured, no more than 10 days would be permitted for recovery, the reasoning being that winter was coming and neither of us would be allowed to jeopardise the expedition for the other. We put the run on hold while David rested for three days. It was the only time we stopped for more than our scheduled rest days on the entire journey. He started off that period of R&R in a seriously negative space, worrying about his ability to continue. I hoped my positive reinforcement was a subconscious seed that would begin to germinate into his own more positive state of mind. The team were all anxious and I'm sure David could pick it up.

On the evening of the third day off, I could tell that David's mindset had changed for the better.

'Let's move on tomorrow,' he said.

His mind had conquered his physical pain. The dream had proved to be bigger than the moment. Of course I was relieved; it takes not only big dreams but big balls to pull off something like this. And of course there were going to be tests to our minds and our bodies. How we each dealt with them would be the proof of what we were made of. It was reassuring to know my partner in this mission had the same determination that I did.

We moved forward again, slowly, and for David, painfully. Doc walked with him as he limped across the desert for the next two days. This gave me time to be alone again, either going ahead or waiting behind, reflecting. It had taken a while longer than we'd planned, but we were moving forward again. That's the thing – having the courage to go forward, even when it hurts … and David did.

17

Paying it Forward

THE INAUGURAL MISSION, or group of operations, for Operation Smile South Africa was taking place in the town of Empangeni in northern KwaZulu-Natal. David's daughter Tamlin and my son Benjamin were both there as volunteers. It was an event that changed both of their young lives as much as running the Great Wall changed mine.

I had phoned Benjamin from my little tent in the desert and heard his quiet, emotional voice explain to me what he had seen and felt. He told me about one boy who was blowing soap bubbles from a little wire hoop for the first time in his life. Before his cleft palate had been repaired, the boy could hardly eat properly and couldn't smile. Now, blowing pretty bubbles, he was smiling with tears in his eyes. Benjamin sounded a little teary too, which rubbed off on me. He told me how he had taken so much for granted, his health, his good looks and the little luxuries most of us accept as a given.

My only sadness was that, while I had seen pictures of some of the children, I could not be present to see and feel the atmosphere. On the up-side, though, it was what we were doing so far away that was helping to make those changes possible. Because of all the volunteers involved, the cost of an average operation was only R5,500 (compared to about ten times that). Even the surgeons and anaesthetists gave up their time and skills for free. They all helped change lives 'one smile at a time'.

Leanne Raymond, PR for our main sponsor Cipla, together with my then-girlfriend Mandi, had organised a Great Wall Challenge Supporters Club. And they did a really great job. Every month or so they would meet at my favourite restaurant, Arnold's in Kloof Street in Cape Town's City Bowl, or have a get-together at my home on Signal Hill. They showed our pictures around, spoke about our blogs and raised money for Operation Smile by selling boerewors rolls and taking pledges.

From one of these gatherings we were phoned in the desert. China is nine hours ahead of South Africa, so it was late at night for us. I chatted first and then woke David so he could talk and answer questions. Benjamin had stood up in front of everyone and told them of his humbling experience with the children. I felt very proud of my son, who was growing up so fast. It felt weird, me at the other end of the world, hearing everyone laughing and cheering and clapping for us. Part of me felt sad and I missed home terribly, but the other part felt elated, proud and not so alone in all of China's alien vastness. Their support meant more than I think they could ever know. Our website, being run by Geoff Smith back in Cape Town, was looking great and the pledges for Operation Smile were picking up nicely. Our weekly blogs kept people up to date with where we were.

Before the start, we had written a charter that stood for what we were doing and what we believed in. Piou translated it into Chinese and the artistic Lee made two beautiful scrolls on special paper. He had them each mounted onto silk with a wooden rod at each end. They were carefully kept in one of the support vehicles by Lunga. He ensured they were signed around the margins by the various party officials in the towns and provinces we passed through. One of the charters was bought on auction at our gala dinner back home by the CEO of Cipla, Jerome Smith, for R100,000. He donated every cent of it to Operation Smile.

The words, I believe, are simple yet profound:

THE CHILDREN'S CHARTER

We, the children of South Africa, call upon our peers and all adults to recognise that every one of the world's children has an equal right to smile, regardless of race, creed, circumstance, fortune, social background, culture or state of health.
This right to smile encompasses:
- *The right to be happy without fear of rejection*
- *The right to be safe and cared for*
- *The right to have friends*
- *The right to laugh without being laughed at*
- *The right to play freely, be active and safe*
- *The right to be treated with dignity and respect*
- *The right to the fullest possible participation in society and the community*
- *The right to interact with the natural environment*
- *The right to believe in and achieve their dreams*
- *The right to fulfil their maximum potential and ability*
- *The right to be self-reliant*

- *The right to enjoy the best attainable state of physical, mental and spiritual health*
- *The right to be seen and heard*

Our declaration:
In order that happiness is freely shared, it is the duty of every child to, whenever possible, pass on a smile to another, in a spirit of mutual support and friendship.

We embrace the three core values of:
- *Respect yourself*
- *Respect others*
- *Respect nature*

The Children's Charter was born out of the fundamental principles and core values of the Great Wall Challenge runners, Braam Malherbe and David Grier, in August 2006.

Natalie Miller and her amazing team at Operation Smile were doing an incredible job back in South Africa. David and I felt really proud of our association with her, Operation Smile and Cipla, not only because we were raising money for them but because we were creating huge awareness amongst the South African public for such an exceptional cause.

When I first met Natalie and discussed taking on Operation Smile as a beneficiary, I spoke to her about my idea of 'paying it forward'. I have worked with underprivileged children for many years and have found that it is often these kids – who usually come from a background of pain and abuse – that rise up beyond circumstance and become tomorrow's leaders. Perhaps it's because they have a greater appreciation of life and their own potential after having experienced hardship and tragedy and learned to move beyond it.

My idea is to select children that have undergone corrective facial surgery and have them sponsored to attend one of the leadership camps I run. In this way they are shown new opportunities and learn to exploit all possibilities in their lives towards realising their dreams. This way the gift they receive in the operation helps to start a whole new life for them. It helps them realise that it's not about looking and being like everyone else, but about contributing to the world in your own, unique, valuable way.

Almost without fail, children who come on these camps go home with an understanding that life is not only about taking but really more about giving. One of the messages I emphasise on the course is that one of the greatest gifts in life is the gift of giving. Children seem to grasp this quite easily. When you are giving to others, to a cause beyond yourself, it leads you to apply your talents and skills with a whole new sort of motivation. When this happens, we naturally grow into people with purpose, and lead richer, more fulfilled lives. I have experienced this myself many times. Whenever you give without an agenda, truly out of love and generosity, you get repaid in other ways many times over in your own life.

In December 1999 devastating fires ravaged the beautiful Table Mountain National Park. As an honorary ranger I could not just watch and do nothing. I rustled up a few of my fitter mates and we went and fought the blaze on our own accord. Then, in early 2000, Jannie du Plessis, a section ranger for the park whom I have known for many years, and Cas Theron, the then head of Fire and Technical Services in Cape Town, asked me if I would be prepared to resuscitate and head the disbanded volunteer fire fighting unit. Just like the honorary rangers, any rewards I received would not be of a financial nature – these were volunteer positions.

The joy and sense of satisfaction I have received as an honorary ranger and volunteer fire fighter over the years have more than made all the work and time invested worthwhile, as well as teaching me valuable skills and helping me grow as a person. I sat on the unit's board as CEO for a number of years, attended many courses in wildfire suppression, including having the privilege of attending the 3rd International Wildfire Conference in Sydney, Australia, with the current head of Fire and Technical Services, Philip Prins, and the head of Fire Management for Cape Nature, Zane Erasmus. I have spent thousands of hours fighting fires in the Table Mountain National Park as well as assisting Cape Nature with training and fire fighting. To help bring a raging wildfire under control and save an area of mountain that is not due for a burn (which should happen only every 10–15 years) truly is priceless.

I remember walking down a narrow zigzag path from the saddle between Table Mountain and Devil's Peak one night after fighting a fire on the mountain for many hours. I had been running up and down the steep gradient through burning vegetation, beating down on flames with a heavy rubber paddle on a long stick called a *plakker* all night, as well as managing my team. I was utterly exhausted. Everything to the right of the path was black and charred, on the left the green vegetation was untouched, thanks to our efforts. We had stopped the blaze and the fire was under control. It must have been about two in the morning and the moon was low in the west.

Pillars of smoke were pouring from the dead land and coals were glowing eerily. The smell of burned earth was everywhere – on my uniform, in my nose and hair. The ground smouldered to the right of the path and trees still burned inside the fire line. The cliffs above looked like shiny melted plastic as they shimmered in the flickering glow. I walked at the back ensuring the safety of my team as they moved ahead of me, eager to get to the safety of the road far below. As I turned a bend, the silver moonlight fell on a perfect orb web of a banded garden spider, its fragile threads spread between the highest twigs of a protea bush just safe to the left of the path, precariously close to where the flames had raged a few hours before.

Hanging upside down in its centre, completely oblivious to how closely it had escaped the inferno, sat the most beautiful yellow and black arachnid. I remember pausing for a moment and feeling the most intense sense of gratitude flow through me. I drank in the peace of the little world in front of me. I felt so privileged that I was instrumental in saving this piece of innocence and I revelled in the beauty of the gift in front of me. This small thing made the biggest difference to me.

The spider thanked me by being a special memory I would never forget, reminding me each time I was suiting up to fight a fire of why I was doing what I was doing. Like seeing a scrub hare run free of the blaze, or a rhino safe in the Kruger National Park, because perhaps the dedicated rangers I had helped train could protect it. 'Paying it forward' for nature has in many ways been in me since I was a child. As I've already said, the sense of satisfaction cannot be measured.

DONGALANDS
Jousting with the Beast

乾裂的土地──與獸搏斗

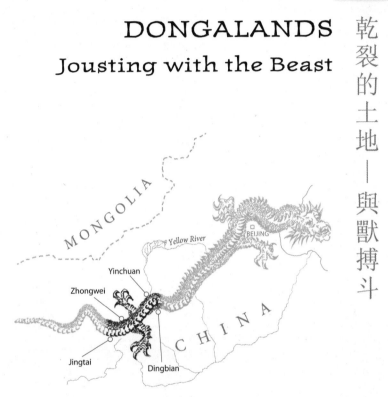

MONGOLIA

Yellow River

BEIJING

Yinchuan

Zhongwei

CHINA

Jingtai

Dingbian

18

Bandits and Birthdays

IT WAS 20 SEPTEMBER and my birthday. I knew, however, that it would be another hard day of running, just like most of the monotonous days of the past few weeks. Or I thought I knew! This confounded place was full of surprises.

The terrain was really harsh. David referred to it as the 'back of the moon'. This was a great description, not only because it was rocky and hilly, but also because it appeared totally devoid of life. I couldn't even spot a plant. The repetitive crunching sound of the brittle, ancient shale underfoot and the smell of flint, sent up from the crushed stone, were all that made me feel I was still there, on Earth. For the rest, I might as well have been on the moon. Tasting my salty sweat, though, made me feel very mortal and human and helped keep me sane.

We were navigating between two broken watchtowers about five kilometres apart and could see our markers only when we were at high points. Then, winding around a steep section of nothingness, I saw smoke. Not like that from a fire or a factory, but literally coming out of the ground. Black and grey smoke billowing into the air from nowhere. As we got closer I realised it was an old deserted coal mine. Literally thousands of mines in the Xinjiang province have been abandoned because of coal fires having been ignited by explosives underground. The fires smoulder along the buried coal seams, inextinguishable. Then I spotted another mine fire about 500 metres to my left.

The raw needs of the rural people in the coal-yielding provinces force them to dig the old abandoned and often extremely dangerous mines. Officially, around 4,000 people die each year in these small mines. Coal pirates also take over many of the abandoned areas, which they control by intimidation and force. The government takes a hard line on them, though, and has vowed to close the many thousands of small mines.

Crunching our way down a hillside, we rounded a boulder and entered a gully. Sticking to the wider track at the base, we jogged around a bend and came slap bang onto a group of four really dodgy looking guys. Slowing to a walk, we gingerly approached the party as we needed to continue past them. It turned out there were more than four, because one of the blokes began shouting in a high-pitched tone down an old mine shaft. Voices echoed up from the black hole. Two of the guys were dressed in trendy, skin-tight denims with scuffed but fancy pointed shoes. They were shirtless and sported black sunglasses. The other two wore boots, jeans and T-shirts. There was a thick old sisal rope dangling over a makeshift wooden scaffold into the abyss.

A souped-up car with silver mag wheels and tinted windows was parked nearby. It looked totally out of place and I wondered how the heck they had got a standard 2×4 vehicle up the rocky gully. Then again, in other places in China we had seen vehicles in the strangest places, so this wasn't something completely new.

'This feels really weird,' I whispered to David.

'Ja, let's just move around them carefully and then get the hell out of here as quickly as possible,' he whispered back.

The ranting from both inside and outside the hole continued, until one of the sleazy characters bellowed and everyone shut up. Clearly the ringleader, he beckoned for us to come closer. By this time, David and I were circling around and slightly above them. It was obvious we were avoiding them. The gang leader began shouting aggressively and kept gesturing for us to come closer.

'For what?' I thought.

Having flanked them and feeling a bit safer, I asked David to take a picture of the coal pirates. He did and all hell broke loose! The two shaded gangster dudes jumped into the car and started reversing as though they were on a tarred road. The other two goons started running up the small embankment after us.

'Geez,' I said. 'Move it *boet*.'

David didn't need my encouragement as we bolted higher up the hillside. Following a narrow goat track, we put on the pace as the two crazies gave chase. I couldn't see the car but could hear the engine whining and wheels grating in the gully somewhere.

'Where're we going?' David shouted.

'Don't know, just run and they won't catch us,' I shouted back.

'I hope they don't have guns,' he said.

That just made me move faster. I looked back and saw we were putting distance between ourselves and the goons, but they showed no signs of stopping the chase. We could no longer hear the car and I began wondering if we were being chased into an ambush; we had no idea where we were but they sure as heck would know the area like the back of their hands. 'Climb,' I wheezed to David just ahead of me.

'Get height so we can get a visual,' I panted.

The guys following us were about half a kilometre behind us by now but were still moving.

'They must have guys ahead or something, otherwise why are they still chasing us?' I said, the sweat now pouring off me.

Reaching a good viewpoint, we could see a jeep track in the valley moving in a long arc away and then curving right back in the direction we were headed. And there was the car, slowly winding its way towards our intended destination of the tower some two kilometres away.

'Let's move west, away from the road,' David suggested. 'They can't catch us in those hills,' he correctly surmised. We ducked down the slope at speed and headed into the wilderness. We went west for two kilometres before curving back towards the next tower. The plan was to end up about a kilometre on the other side of it.

'They don't have guns,' I guessed, as we traced another gully, now walking, 'or they would have used them long ago.'

'Maybe not,' said David. 'Shots could give them away.'

Private guns are banned in China. Only police and military carry them. A civilian caught with a gun faces the death penalty. The thought made me feel a little better.

After passing east of the tower, I sent an SMS to Hans asking for their GPS position. The hills were getting higher and steeper. Entering the co-ordinates, Garmin told us they were only three crow-fly kilometres away. It didn't make sense: how could they be ahead when there was only rocky terrain with steep hills?

'There must be a track or something,' David said.

Vodacom SA had sponsored a vital chunk of airtime and I decided to use some of it to call Hans.

'Ja, zerr is a road here in ze mountains,' he confirmed.

I told him what had happened and warned him to be on the lookout, as the hoods would also know of the road.

'I hope zey come!' barked Hans. He was a tough guy and a member of the Austrian army's permanent force.

By 13h00 when we crested a ridge and saw the gravel road, the day was hot, at least 35 °C, and I was thoroughly pissed off.

'Some birthday,' I muttered to myself as I pulled off my shoes.

We never saw the 'baddies' again.

Hans and Doc Michael met us at the lunch stop and told us the rest of the team had gone ahead to find a good campsite.

The afternoon's terrain was much the same as what we had covered in the morning, although it looked like we were moving into more open land, as the hills were becoming rounded and gentle, with occasional shrubs appearing. We passed another four towers and a small piece of Wall comprising eroded mud mixed with rock. Millions of camels had carted water in urns and pig-skin bladders into the remote dry regions to build the Wall. Here, the water was mixed with the chalky, pale orange earth to make the mud that was compacted, layer upon layer. Looking at the landscape all around me, I could hardly imagine it.

'Crazy,' I thought, feeling very happy to be living in South Africa in the 21st century.

David was jogging ahead when suddenly he did this cute little dance, arms out sideways, as he pirouetted off the path.

'Whaaaa!' he screamed.

I immediately saw the snake moving fast across the trail and gave chase. Since I was a young kid I've been fascinated by snakes. My dad had collected them when he was a boy and my deceased uncle Dan had shown me how to catch them when I was around seven years old. I loved the respect they commanded from us 'apex predators'.

'Don't get bitten,' cautioned David, who has a serious fear of the reptiles. 'There's no-one here to help you, just leave it alone,' he said, knowing me well enough to realise that his words fell on deaf ears.

The snake was very thin and agile. It went into a low bush and vanished. I knew it had to be there, so I approached the bush slowly. It was frozen still, lying well camouflaged. I moved my hand very slowly while David stood at a safe distance. Then I lunged at the snake, quickly grabbing it. I pulled it free of the bush and slid it under my foot, being careful not to harm the animal. I gently got it around the neck and held it up to get a proper look.

'Beautiful,' I said, 'what a birthday present!'

■ **TOP:** Eroded mud Wall stretches across the desert like a dried-out millipede.
LEFT: Dead ends in the Donga-lands really messed with my head.
ABOVE RIGHT: We walked right into a military training ground – dummy land mines and all.

■ **ABOVE:** The dust storm cometh.
BELOW: Celebrating my birthday in the Gobi desert was a wonderful, colourful and intercultural experience.
BELOW LEFT: Lee's beautiful handwritten charters mounted on silk.

■ **THIS PAGE:** Near-death experiences, like getting caught in a dust storm and almost drowning in quicksand, proved to be extremely humbling.

■ **THIS SPREAD:** The haunting beauty of the Wall was inspiring and continually lifted my spirits.

■ **THIS PAGE:** The never-ending inclines and declines were relentless and tested my body and mind to the limit. In the end, the uphills, put back to back, equalled the height of Mount Everest 14.8 times.

■ THIS PAGE: The big chill: For me, the crux of the long, hard months was the biting cold. Putting on four layers of clothing in the confines of my small tent, I would need to get my head right before opening the zip and stepping into each freezing day.

ABOVE: Leaving the tourist Wall and entering 'no-man's land'.

ABOVE RIGHT: Having fun on one of our rest days: me in Chinese military 'disguise'.

■ The cold was seriously debilitating.
TOP: Resting in the sun on the Loess plateau.
LEFT: Crossing frozen rivers very nearly led to disaster.
MIDDLE RIGHT: A modern day 'Wall builder'. These folks cart old bricks, which were taken to build villages, back up the mountains to reconstruct the Wall. They get paid a pittance.

It really was beautiful. It looked like a species of whip snake that is common in desert areas. If handled incorrectly they can give a nasty bite, but their venom is weak, usually causing nothing more than a mild headache. They feed predominantly on lizards. David took a picture of my birthday present before I gave it back its freedom and we moved forward with our day's task. It wasn't more than 100 metres before David saw another snake and treated me to another hilarious sidestep. I called it his hieroglyphic dance because he 'walked like an Egyptian'. I pissed myself laughing as I re-enacted his dance. He took it well and, as we walked and laughed together, asked me to run in front. No idea why! We moved over the brow of a hill and saw the green tents in a wide, open plain.

'Home,' we both said, almost simultaneously.

I had asked Lunga to instruct the crew to always put my tent at least 100 metres upwind from everyone else. I had lived in near isolation at Appleton Camp on Signal Hill above Cape Town for more than 20 years. My closest neighbour was two and a half kilometres away and I was used to silence. I loved it, but any noise woke me, especially another member of the team snoring loudly! When I was woken, my head filled with thoughts of home, the day ahead and, often, mistakes I'd made in my past. I would lie awake, wrestling with that past and try to fix it in my head. I struggled to get back to sleep, all the time telling myself I must, because I needed to rest to be strong the next day. Being upwind, with earplugs firmly inserted, helped a lot. So, walking into camp, I simply looked for the tent furthest away from the others and went to my room.

I used the pee-pot-size plastic fold-up bath to wash. First my face, then one leg at a time, then crouch, splash water under my right arm, change, splash under my left arm, squat, and do the rest. If David got to it first, I would make a hole in the sand, place a black garbage bag in it, fill it with water and do pretty much the same thing. Then I'd escape to the quiet and solitude of my tent.

There may have been chattering outside but I was alone in my own world. My bare feet, all white against my hectic sock tan, would be perched together in the little noose dangling from the roof of the tent, like crooning doves come home to roost in the nest of my smelly socks, placed carefully over the noose as a cushion for my tender, tired feet. With my hands on my chest, I'd close my eyes and breathe quiet thanks for another day accomplished and, on this particular day, for my life.

My eyes closed as the late afternoon sun filtered through the right side of my tent. I could smell the desert and me; chalky dust and my sleeping bag. The bag smelled of my body; dusty with desert powder, with a scent of salt, but was warm, almost sensual and safe. I was really happy to be alive.

'Mr Braam, Mr Braam,' called Little Chang softly, close to my tent.

'Jaaa?' I slurred back, in a melancholic half-doze.

'You must come outside now, please?' he said.

'Oh no, not another blasted meeting,' I sighed to myself, and then 'Okay' to Chang.

I unzipped the insect netting inner and slipped my feet into my slops lying just inside the fly-sheet. Before I could stand up from the tent, Little Chang leaned forward and presented me with some desert flowers in a *pijou* bottle that Doc Michael had conveniently emptied for the occasion.

'Happy birsday,' he said, showing off his customary special smile.

The entire team, David included, was standing outside my tent. Doc with his piano accordion and Hans with his guitar began playing 'Happy Birthday' for me. After great applause, I finally got out of the tent and stood up. What a special and totally unexpected surprise! But it was not over yet.

Lilly called me over to the little camp table and there, in the middle, was a stunning birthday cake with icing flowers and 'happy birthday Braam' written on it. Next to the cake was a bottle of whisky. While whisky was my preferred alcoholic beverage, I had not had any since leaving Cape Town and was a little hesitant to sip down the way-more-than-a-tot that half filled a plastic cup next to the bottle. Needless to say, we all polished off the bottle of disgusting Chinese-made stuff. Even David had some. He had not even touched a *pijou* since we'd started our journey. It was certainly not whisky, no matter how much Lunga earnestly argued that it was 'finest whiski, finest whiski'.

After Lilly had placed a paper party crown on each of our heads it was time for the party trick, which clearly was on me! Lilly cut the cake and presented everyone with a healthy portion on a colourful paper plate. As she was about to hand me mine, she suddenly shoved the whole sticky slice slap in my face. The entire crew collapsed as Lunga and Lilly smeared the mess into my hair.

David was the designated cameraman. Trying to clean the goo off with cold water was a mission. Eventually, Lilly boiled some water on the gas stove, which I used to clean myself up.

There was a small rocky hill next to the camp. David, Hans and I climbed to the top for a last *'prost'* of the dubious liquid. Then, in our emboldened states, we dropped our shorts and offered the crew our naked butts by way of thanks. Unfortunately cameras were at the ready. Lee has since brought out a book in Chinese about our journey along the Great Wall and there, for all of China to see, is a full-colour picture of three naked butts, with me peering between my legs still wearing my crown. Great ambassador!

It turned out that when Michael and Hans were at our lunch GPS position, the rest of the crew were on an 80-kilometre round trip to organise the cake and the 'whisky'. It was a birthday I will never forget and it was with people I will never forget. David had even put on a dance for me, twice!

Around nightfall a light wind picked up and my fly-sheet flapped as I lay in my tent in the darkness. I could hear Michael playing soulful tunes on his guitar in the distance.

'Hey Michael, will you play me that Bob Dylan number I like?' I called out hopefully. And so an exciting and special day ended as I dozed listening to *'How many roads must a man walk down, before you can call him a man; How many seas must a white dove sail, before she sleeps in the sand...? The answer, my friend, is blowin' in the wind, the answer is blowin' in the wind.'*

Needless to say, the next day was a slower start and a slower pace.

'That was definitely not whisky,' I said, my head throbbing.

'No ways,' agreed David, who had had hardly more than a tot and was feeling way better than I was.

I was grateful it was a lot flatter as we followed the remnants of the Wall across a massive open plain, cut here and there by deep dongas. After about 10 kilometres we came across a barbed-wire fence with white cement posts. Following the fence line, it eventually cut through a broken section of Wall, which we clambered over. We had seen the occasional red sign on a white background wired to the fence, but clearly had no idea what they said (although the intent was not hard to figure). With the fence long gone and the terrain becoming more undulating, we came across wide bulldozer-like tracks, then more, then lots of them.

'There's no construction anywhere in sight,' David observed.

'I wonder what they're from?' I asked, somewhat rhetorically. Then I noticed a scattering of rounded white-topped lumps about the size of large dinner plates ahead. Suddenly all the pieces came together.

'Oh shit, we're in a military zone,' I said. 'Those are land mines up ahead and those tracks back there are from tanks.'

It wasn't a joke. We approached the mines cautiously, wondering why they were exposed. On closer inspection they turned out to be compacted sand, obviously made from a mould to imitate land mines. We were slap in the middle of a training ground. The hills to the left were riddled with bunkers and trenches. I didn't need to understand Chinese to know what the signs on the fence had meant: 'Keep out or else!'

'We better get a GPS message soon,' I said.

'Getting caught here could be a serious problem,' replied David.

There were hills to our left and open plains to our right. The Wall hugged the base of the hills.

'If we stick between the Wall and the hills we won't be spotted,' said David, as we picked up our pace.

'Good call,' I agreed.

Then I saw huge potholes. I stopped to pick up a piece of metal.

'It's shrapnel, we're running through a heavy artillery firing range. Geez, I hope it's their day off,' I said between breaths.

I wasn't sure if we were running deeper into trouble or away from it. We just followed the Wall and hoped for the best. I spotted something towards the horizon shimmering in the blazingly hot sun. I stopped to check it out with my binos. It was three flatbed trailers on a rail track. Mounted on the flatbeds were three very big guns. We were running parallel to the rail track, about two kilometres from them, alongside broken sections of the Wall, dodging potholes that had been created by the artillery fire.

'Great!' I thought, my headache long forgotten.

After a very tense and fast 12 kilometres, we climbed over another fence to relative safety.

'Hell, couldn't Lunga have found out about this?' I moaned. 'If we had got caught up in a fire exercise, it could have been the end of the expedition – and us. The crew has to split up and recce a day ahead,' I reiterated.

David and I had discussed this on numerous occasions and suggested it to Lunga via the interpreter Piou but, apart from a lot of polite nodding, nothing had happened. It was now coming to a head. We decided to not discuss it that evening, but rather put it on the agenda for our next rest-day debriefing.

19

Footsore

THE PAIN UNDER MY FEET WAS GETTING WORSE. Sometimes I would need to stop, take off my shoes and pull my toes and forefoot back hard in order to stretch the tendon under my arch. If I didn't do it for long enough, my foot would cramp so badly I thought the tendon might snap. I asked Doc to check it out again. There was nothing visibly amiss, but he said it was really tight. I used some of the anti-inflammatory cream that Cipla had given us and massaged it into my arch every lunch time and every evening, slowly running my thumb along its length, trying to stretch it. Doc said I'd need to do it every day for a week or two.

It seemed to work a bit, but the daily pain under my feet persisted. It felt like I was running on sharp stones, which caused my feet to become ultra-sensitive. I changed my shoe-exchange pattern from weekly to daily. I had 10 pairs with numbers written on the tongues. Today would be pair one, tomorrow pair two and so on. It didn't make any difference. It wasn't my Adidas shoes that were at the root of the problem, because I had suffered the same pain on both my two previous long runs and I had used different shoes on each occasion. I just had to grin and bear it, one day at a time, one step at a time.

David's monster heel blister was by now so big I used my Leatherman knife to cut away the heel of his shoe to take the pressure off. After two days of getting sand in the hole, he decided to 'slay the monster'. Doc lanced it with a heated knife and strapped it. After a few days David was smiling.

'I feel like I'm running on air,' he said. I wished I felt the same.

We were somewhere south of Yulin. The going was tough as the weeks wore on. They didn't take their toll only on our bodies, but also on our minds. Both our tempers were getting shorter and we started to get ratty with one another. We still had a long way to go and yet already I felt unable to express myself freely to David. He appeared sullen a lot of the time and I was building anger inside. I also wanted to be on my own. So did David.

Some days, after a short, snappy answer to a simple question, we would create a bit of distance between us. Often he would run on one side of the Wall and I would run on the other. We had agreed at the beginning that we would always remain in either eye or vocal contact. So every hour or so I would hear 'How goes it?' from the other side of the wall. Occasionally I would shout 'You cool?'

And that's how we got through some of the hard days as we neared the middle of our epic. I knew we needed to discuss the deeper issues. I was suppressing a lot of concerns that would turn to anger if not dealt with. That could jeopardise things and I wanted to avoid anything that might put me or the expedition at risk. Clinton, our psychologist back in South Africa, had said how important it would be to communicate effectively. I was surprised how seemingly small, almost insignificant things would gnaw at us and build into potentially debilitating problems. This was largely because of the compound effects of daily physical and mental stress, coupled with the fact that we were basically in each other's presence every waking hour. By the end of the expedition we would have spent more than 900 hours together. It was not until we were in the cold in the high mountains, however, that things would finally come to a head. It would also bring us closer.

We were way past the 1,000-kilometre mark where we had all sat on a sand dune with a huge '1,000 km' and a smiley face drawn in the sand. It seemed so long ago, almost a dream. The days were not as hot anymore and the nights were now getting really cold. It was early October and my son Ben's birthday was coming up. One afternoon I saw a beautiful tree at an oasis and decided to sketch it for him as a gift. The main trunk was stout where it came out of the soil. Two young offshoots stretched out from the base of the trunk, nurtured by shade and water drawn from deep below the desert sands.

It reminded me of the story I often share with children at my nature camps. I stand next to a tall old tree. 'This is like your parent,' I say as I firmly hold the trunk. 'Stable, anchored, nourishing you by feeding you from their roots and sheltering you with their shade. But, like many parents, it has grown in a certain way and has become rather inflexible.'

Reaching up, I grab a branch: 'This is you,' I explain. 'You are still attached to the tree but you are also still very flexible. This is good, because if you recognise your flexibility, you can make healthy choices about the direction you want to take.'

Benjamin was still young but he was fast becoming a man. He would be turning 18 on 8 October and was not as attached to the 'trunk' as he used to be. The sketch I did for him was so appropriate: the young sapling slowly finding its own way while knowing the parent is still close by if needed.

My friends Shelly and Hugh Knyvet-Knevitt had offered their home to Benjamin while I was in China. I was very grateful as Benjamin was friends with their two sons Dane and Byron. Also, Ben saw Shelly almost as a second mom. I had discussed Ben's living arrangements with his real mom Berit before going to China. Although divorced, we have learned to communicate openly regarding our past and our son. As we both matured over the years, we have learned a new respect for one another. While he enjoyed visiting his mom, she lived too far away from his school for it to be practical for Benjamin to live with her. She had also recently had a baby, which was not conducive to Ben doing his homework effectively. I also knew Shelly could be both nurturing and firm when necessary. Mac was also a great support for Benjamin and would often have him stay over on weekends. So, all in all, I felt comfortable that my son was in good hands.

Heading towards Yulin and the Loess plateau, we were on the 2,000-kilometre mark. The days had become monotonous and progressively colder. They dragged slowly into weeks and the weeks were now becoming months. After almost two months on the arid interior plateau I had begun to think there was no other world – only hard-baked ochre earth. The daily grind had become a painful habit. The lonely days hid haunting ghosts – memories playing over and over in my mind.

Lying in my tent, tucked into my sleeping bag through the cold nights, I would slowly peel off the layers of clothing, one at a time, as my body heated up in its insulated down cocoon. Sometimes I would lie reading in the white glare from my head lamp, or other times I'd just think in the inky blackness. Often I would be woken from a restless sleep by the howling desert wind tugging at my tent. I felt I was a tiny creature, trapped inside a paper bag in the wilderness; the only things keeping me tethered were small pins for tent pegs. I would just lie there, not moving, waiting for the morning and a new day to run.

In the cold, grey dawn I would dress inside my sleeping bag, open my tent and run into another day, and another time. I was on a desolate planet – barren and devoid of life. At least that's how it felt sometimes. When I was fatigued or in pain, or when I felt really alone, the wasteland echoed those emotions.

When I started in the desert, so long ago, I would see a bird – a red rock kestrel – swoop from the ocean-cool blue sky, and be reminded of the life around me. In those first weeks I would feel the life in the wind. I would see the living shadows of the bushes dance in the afternoon breeze. Even my skin's salty sweat was alive; everything seemed magnified, larger than life.

But now I'd had enough of it. As endless barren, rocky hills and tricky dongas stretched to the horizon it felt as if the mountains would never come.

'They are an illusion,' I said to David. 'Just mud Wall, sand and crumbling rocks and stone,' I moaned.

In truth we were very close to the western edge of the arid interior plain and close approaching the Lüliang Shan, the real mountains.

'And it's getting colder,' David replied.

And so we had passed the 2,000-kilometre mark, but the hardest part of the journey still lay ahead: high mountains, cold winds, shorter days, ice and snow. Although the days would get tougher, I still yearned for the mountains. I had always loved the high places. I had learned all I could from the dry, cracked lowlands ... or so I thought.

20

A Private Wall

THE ARID, GNARLED LOESS PLATEAU that we were now crossing – the place we had dubbed the Dongalands – is a deceptive place. Mirages play games with your mind and distances are distorted by hills and gullies.

The plateau was hugely fertile in ancient times and led to the development of early Chinese civilisation. However, it is also extremely prone to erosion and, with cultivation, the winds of the region quickly stripped away the topsoil to leave it bare and brutal.

Loess, often used as a term for any wind-deposited sand, has been classified as the most erodible soil on the planet. We thought we would meet the team for lunch, but the terrain was too rough and they couldn't get close enough to the broken Wall. Now, as we moved toward our support crew at the end of a long and very undulating day, Garmin told me we had only 2.2 kilometres to go. The hills in the twilight seemed to stretch on forever.

I calculated the team would be over the next ridge. As I crested the rise the ground fell away near vertically. Below me, some 200 metres steeply down, was what looked like red mud with pools here and there. The small white dots I could see were goats. There appeared no way down and the light was fading fast. I moved down a crumbling, narrow gully and picked up faint goat tracks. Following them was our best chance. The dry sand cliff was brittle and clumps of it would break away and tumble in balls of dust to the valley below. Using our trekking poles for bracing and to test the ground ahead before stepping on it, we crabbed our way down at a painfully slow pace. The dark gloom below was uninviting. I paused for a few minutes, using the remaining light to plot an escape route up the other side.

Finally, reaching the bottom, I put on my head lamp. David hadn't packed his because we thought we would arrive at camp well before sundown – which was to be another hard lesson learned. Apart from our standard kit, we decided to thereafter always carry an emergency blanket, basic first-aid kit, 10-metre safety line, matches, knife, a candle, head lamp and spare batteries.

The bottom of the gully comprised thick mud with smelly pools scattered about. Testing the mud's consistency with my trekking pole, I realised it was not solid enough to support my body weight without my feet being sucked in and, anyway, we needed dry shoes to climb up the also near vertical cliff on the other side. So yet another frustrating delay as we removed shoes and socks, moved across the ankle-deep bog, removed the mud with our socks and put our shoes back on minus socks. I went up first, about 10 metres, so I could light the way, and also because of David's fear of heights. He slipped and fell as the dry, caked earth broke away from under him; thank God it was only in the first few metres. From then on I used my poles to gouge out holes for foot placements, before bracing myself and shining the beam for David. I repeated the process, making footholds all the way. It was laborious but safe. It took us over an hour to climb 200 metres back out and by then it was dark – very dark.

According to Garmin, we had a mere 600 metres to go, but there were no lights in sight. Trundling on we found a 4×4 track, which led off our bearing to the right. I could see fresh vehicle tracks so we decided to follow them. The 600-metre crow-fly on Garmin was 1.4 kilometres on the ground before we saw the flashing torch beacon on good old Lunga's vehicle.

It had been a very long, tiring and frustrating day. We had covered a punishing 58 kilometres, but it read only 24 linear ones! We did a quicker-than-usual stretch before chucking our kit into the Toyota 4×4 and driving off to Lee's home village for a much-anticipated rest day. David and I shared a 'hotel' room, which consisted of two mattresses on a concrete floor. The window didn't even have a curtain and there was a bright street light right outside the window.

'At least we can grab a hot shower,' I said to David. 'You go first, just leave me some hot water.'

The shower was at the end of the passage. David was back in less than five minutes. 'So much for that,' he said irritably, 'there's only a trickle and it's freezing.'

He kindly gave me a packet of Wet Wipes. He had brought a whole bunch of them from South Africa and they were really prized articles, especially for cleaning in the confines of a small tent.

Wiping the mud off my feet, I watched myself as though in slow motion. Quite suddenly I felt really whacked. I had an out-of-body feeling and didn't want to do anything except sleep. It was a sign I recognised all to well – hypoglycaemia – and realised my body urgently needed food. My body had simply run out of blood sugar and therefore energy. I had pushed hard all day, keeping focused in a tricky situation with not enough fuel to run at those high revs. Thinking we had a relatively easy day ahead, I had eaten a full breakfast but had packed only three energy bars. I had missed lunch and was running on adrenaline by the end of the day. This was exactly what Tim Noakes and Shelly Meltzer had meant when they had cautioned us about following the right nutrition, and the need to eat regularly.

'Remember to force yourself to eat when you are tired or cold,' Shelly had said back in Cape Town.

I just wanted to sleep but knew I should eat first to aid my body's recovery. The team was at a restaurant down the road.

'Come, let's go, we need to eat,' said David, clearly feeling stronger than me.

We joined the crew for a quick soup at a grimy noodle bar. The walls were greasy with grey mould in places, making impressive patterns in the corners. The tables were covered with either bright red, blue or green plastic nailed down at the corners. The nails had accumulated dark, greasy deposits around the heads where the wiping clothes couldn't get to. Steam was coming out of the kitchen and the place smelled of a mixture of chillies and curry powder. One of the chefs came out from the noisy kitchen to gawk at the foreigners. It looked as though he hadn't washed his outfit, ever! 'Don't judge noodle soup by the décor,' was an expression we had used a good few times. The soup was fantastic and gave me the boost I needed. Back in the 'no-star' hotel, I rolled out my sleeping bag on the stained mattress, jammed in my earplugs and tried to dream of home.

Thank goodness, after the hectic 58-kilometre day, the next day was a rest one. We were in Lee's home town of An Bian, about 40 kilometres out of the city of Yulin. So, after e-mailing, writing a blog and washing socks (no-one, not even a laundromat, would wash our socks in China, it simply wasn't done: underwear yes, socks no) we went off to Lee's house to meet 'the family' and have lunch. What a surprise it turned out to be! This quiet gentleman who, like Little Chang, always smiled, was also an exceptional artist, photographer and historian. He gestured for David and me to follow him up a short flight of stairs. I stood in awe as I looked at his sacred space. It was like seeing Lee for the first time. Although I had realised a month earlier he was passionate about photography and the Great Wall,

I had not thought much further on it. It was difficult anyway, with a large crew and being tired most of the time, to really get to know any one of the crew in great depth. Also, none of the Chinese members except for Piou spoke any English.

I stood in the well-lit room and stared at his studio and private Chang Cheng (Great Wall) museum. Along one wall ran a long shelf of perhaps five metres. It was adorned with pieces of pottery, arrow heads, inscriptions in baked clay, an old hand grenade and even a small piece of chain mail from a long-gone soldier. These were artefacts and relics Lee had picked up on his many solitary excursions along the Wall. The Wall had been in his blood since he was a child. It was in him still; he was as passionate as ever. Another smaller shelf had a row of bones and animal skulls. Lee was also a naturalist, it appeared. Later Piou explained that Lee had seen many of these animals, mainly small antelope, as a youngster.

'But there is nothing now, all gone,' he concluded.

Covering the wall behind his large artist's table was a beautiful water-colour of the mud towers stretching out along the desert. And all around were scattered black-and-white photographs of the Great Wall and Lee.

I guess what amazed me the most, what I really identified with, was the man's obsession. He had found a large part of his identity living in the shadow of the Wall. He had climbed many a tower and looked left and right along its snaking length and felt his own history. Starting from his boyhood wanderings was born a passion; not only had he studied the history of the Wall, through it he had discovered his own ancestors. Lee lived in an insignificant, remote, Third World village in the middle of nowhere (even though there was a city just 40 kilometres away). But he dreamed still and, fuelled by this passion, he was living out his dream by journeying the length of the Wall – in a different way to me but just as real.

David and Lee had gone downstairs. I walked slowly around his sacred space, touching priceless things, looking at old pictures covered in dust and smelling the desert whenever I blew the dust off to get a better look at something. I liked this man a lot. He seemed like such an old soul. I went downstairs and joined the group. The tablecloth was an array of newspapers scattered over the table. It wasn't meant to look good; this experience was all about taste.

Lee's wife was an attractive woman and she wore a bright red jersey that showed off her shining black hair. We sat on stools around the table while she brought in one dish after another. Bowls of peeled cloves of garlic, which are a regular feature at most meals, chillies, tea-eggs and corn adorned the table. These were dipped into the soup or mixed with fine rice noodles.

I noticed how Lee's wife held her chopsticks high up the shafts. Piou had told me it was a sign of wealth or aristocracy. The rest of us held them much lower down. It was certainly a lot easier. Only bottles with liquid in them were permitted on the table and if anyone's plastic cup was empty, it was hastily refilled with *pijou* and loud '*gambeys*' were toasted with cups held high. '*Che che*' and '*bukatchi*' – 'thank you' and 'you're welcome' – were the most popular words after '*gambey*'. Many empty quart bottles of *pijou* already stood on a shelf against one wall, testament to a good time.

Then the meat arrived. No donkey or pig today. Instead an entire sheep had been slaughtered in our honour. There were no plates but bowls. The meat was presented in chunks with skin and fat all piled together. The idea was to grab a piece in your hands and eat it, discarding any bones on the newspaper tablecloth. It was a really delicious but seriously messy affair. It reminded me of a medieval banquet, with Michael and Hans playing accordion and guitar as the travelling minstrels. After green tea and way too much food and *pijou*, my eyes started drooping. I hadn't slept very well the previous night, constantly being woken by a drunken, excessively loud group of people playing cards upstairs until who knew what time.

When Lunga opened a bottle of rice wine I took the opportunity to excuse myself quietly from the party. I wrote a bit until I was sleepy and then had a really good two-hour nap. That evening some of us met at the local grease bar for soup. We discussed the terrain ahead. Lee had said it was very broken ground with lots of mud and sludge in the valleys. We just needed to look for towers to follow, as the Wall was barely visible in places because of the badly eroded landscape. Before bed, David and I packed carefully for what looked to be a long tomorrow as we headed into the foothills.

THE FOOTHILLS

Entering the Dragon's Lair

山丘（黄土高原）—— 進入龍穴

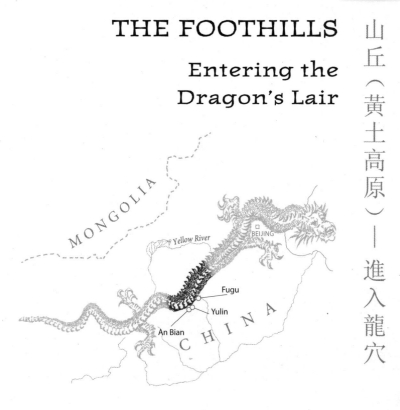

21

Drowning

DRIVING BACK THROUGH THE HILLY GROUND to the last GPS point we had got to in the dark before rest day, I could see clearly just how badly eroded the land was. This terrain was seriously adding unnecessary extra kilometres to our journey. Little did we know that the mountains were to increase our actual distances even more. The ground was becoming increasingly steep with a mixture of ancient, caked earth interspersed with rocky outcrops making progress slow and difficult.

The day was cloudless and with no wind, but autumn was fast sliding into winter and it was −10 °C when we started out at 07h00. We had decided never to start or finish again in the dark if we could help it. A head lamp throws long shadows behind an obstacle or rock, particularly on declines, and it becomes difficult to know if it is just a shadow or a hole, so you have to go at a much slower pace than you would otherwise to avoid injury. This leads to frustration, which again increases the chance of injury.

Even at 07h00 it was still not quite light enough to run so we usually walked the first few kilometres, especially on the sort of jumbled terrain we were crossing. I suspected we would be doing a lot more walking, even climbing and crawling, during the next few weeks. Things were starting to get a whole lot tougher.

By lunch time we had covered around 35 kilometres, but less than half that in a straight line: up, down, up, down, wrong turn, no escape, go back. I was really frustrated, but knew from experience it was important to just take it one donga at a time. Scrambling and sliding down a steep 200-metre embankment, I arrived at yet another insipid little umber, muddy stream. It was only about five metres across, but it still meant removing shoes – again.

Both sides had a wide and what looked like solid flood-plain shoulder, which then dropped about a metre down to a shiny, smooth muddy flank about 50 metres wide. David was just as frustrated as I was and decided to follow the bank upstream in the hope of finding a narrower section to jump across without having to remove his shoes. He took a photo of me crossing the muddy, sticky ooze that constituted the stream bank. Good thing this wasn't being videoed, because what was coming out of my mouth was not viewer-friendly stuff!

Trying to walk along the far bank was almost impossible. The mud had set to a jelly-like substance. Initially it held my weight when I stood on it, it wobbled a bit, then collapsed, sucking my foot in with a loud slurp. I went down to about halfway up my calf. Then the next foot: stand, apply pressure to pull my stuck foot out and 'slurp', in went my other foot. My trekking poles were useless here, as they just went right in like a fork into mashed potato.

Eventually, after a good 15 minutes of this, I hauled my very muddy self onto what looked like a drier and less gooey surface than the muck I had just waded through. It seemed to support my weight as I gingerly tested the ground. After a couple of metres I felt a little more confident and started moving a bit faster towards the higher bank, now just 10 metres ahead. The ground suddenly moved under me. It seemed to dent downwards as if I was standing on a very softly sprung trampoline. Then the surface broke and the muck swallowed me right up to my waist. I instinctively tried to lean my body weight forward, holding both my trekking poles with as wide a 'footprint' as I could, but I was still going deeper, as if in slow motion.

I screamed at the top of my voice: 'Help,' I shouted, 'David, help, I'm in the shit!'

I had fallen through a semi-dry crust about 15 centimetres thick. Below that was a sticky liquid about the consistency of honey and the thick mess was flowing very slowly under the caked surface. I couldn't pull myself out. Luckily my backpack and trekking poles were keeping me buoyed up, but I knew it would not be for much longer.

I screamed again. 'Where are you?'

I heard David shouting from somewhere behind me.

'Here, over here, hurry, hurry,' I screamed in panic.

I could feel my feet being pulled slowly but insistently downstream. The slowness and determination of the sucking motion was frightening, mainly because it gave me time to think about the kind of slow death that would most certainly follow if I wasn't rescued soon.

'Oh shit!' David shouted, when he saw how little of me was left sticking out of the mud.

'Don't walk on that hard stuff, it isn't hard,' I shouted back. It's weird how we shout when we panic. I remember thinking that in the middle of my crisis. We could have whispered and heard each other perfectly well.

David pulled out his 10-metre safety rope.

'Grab the rope,' he said.

But there was no way he could physically pull me out. There was nothing solid to anchor to.

'Push your poles into the mud,' I screamed at him in a panic, 'as deep as you can, about half a metre apart. Push down with your body till they won't go in any more.'

I had twirled the end of the safety line around one of my wrists as well as around my poles.

'Now what?' he asked, but he was already looping the safety line around the poles.

'Figure eights,' I shouted, by now deep enough to be tasting mud and pulling on the rope. 'Figure eights.'

'Stop pulling, just stop pulling for a mo …,' he screamed back. 'Okay, now pull,' he urged.

And I did, except I didn't move – but neither did the anchor poles. I pulled again. I moved a fraction, so pulled again. The poles held fast. I pulled again, winding the rope around my right wrist with every pull. I felt like a worm being pulled from a very tight hole. Except a more-than-willing worm.

It took at least 20 minutes before I managed to pull myself free of the river. My feet were encased in a ball of mud, all stuck together like a Mafia victim with his feet in a cement block that hadn't quite set. I leopard-crawled as fast as I could across the mud to safety, looking more like a slug than a leopard. David grabbed my wrist 'monkey grip' and dragged me up the slope.

'Geez,' I said, and then I really swore. 'What the fuck just happened there? I nearly died, really slowly,' I panted.

'But you didn't,' David said, also panting.

Getting most of the mud off took a good half hour. By then we had both calmed down, talking very quietly, almost in whispers, when we spoke.

We moved on towards the end of the day, each in his own reflective space. Still now I remember the silence of that afternoon, more than any other. I can remember once again feeling a deep sense of gratitude. I also felt very vulnerable and small. On the one hand I was trying to do something amazing, while on the other I knew it could all end very quickly, maybe even horribly. The sun was a deep tangerine as it hung low above the horizon. I thought about how many times in my life I had escaped death. I recalled the time I had almost drowned in a really stupid accident in Cape Town harbour.

Having completed my military stint I had become a commercial diver. After I had done some repair work under a ship one day, another diver, Allan Stephens, arrived to do a job under another ship. He asked me to leave the truck that had the compressor on the back with him, and for me to drive his car back to the workshop.

'Just watch the brakes,' he said, 'they're a bit dodge, so pump them first.'

After pumping the foot brake, which initially went flat to the floor but then gave some resistance, I started to reverse the vehicle between two cranes. I pushed the brake ... but nothing happened. I pumped furiously as the car continued rolling slowly backward towards the edge of the jetty. Still nothing happened. I pulled the hand brake, but it wasn't connected and came away in my hand! By that stage it was too late to jump out as the back wheels had dropped over the edge.

After that, everything happened way too quickly. The car went over backwards, I fell into the back seat, the windscreen and front of the roof crunched in on the mooring lines of the ship and broke inwards. When the back of the car hit the green, oily water, the impact caused it to bounce and fall back onto its roof.

'Get out, get out,' I was saying to myself as the panic rushed into my body at the same rate as the water pouring into the cab.

The underwater work I had been doing was extremely demanding and I had been running on adrenaline, with no time to think about anything other than the absolute focus of the task. Afterwards, dressed in an overall and gumboots, I had felt drained. Now I was totally disorientated and had no idea where I was in the vehicle. It felt as though I was in a washing machine as the water poured in through the smashed windscreen. I couldn't do anything as the car rapidly filled with pale green sea water. I remember just holding onto a seat or something.

When the cab was full it started sinking rapidly because I remember how dark it got suddenly. I ran my hands along the edge of the back door and groped for the window winder. I could feel my heart pounding like a hammer in my chest, as though it also wanted to get out. I wound down the window in the dark murk and pulled myself through. Looking up, I remember how far away the light flare on the surface seemed to be. My gumboots came off easily as I shook them loose and pushed hard for the air above. My lungs couldn't hold out any longer and as I gasped for air water poured in.

'I'm not ready to die, I'm not going to die, I have things to do,' I scolded myself in a rising panic.

People with no experience will tell you drowning is a peaceful experience. But let me tell you there was nothing peaceful about what I was experiencing. Gagging on water, I broke the surface, spluttering and vomiting as I sucked in the life-giving air. On the front page of the local newspaper the next day there was a colour picture of Allan and me standing in front of a very stuffed-up Hillman Vogue. I was smiling but Allan wasn't.

Walking towards the day's end I could see the camp tents, no more than one kilometre away, silhouetted against the now-crimson sun as it began dipping below the horizon. So many times in my life I had been perilously close to death but come out alive on the other side, I pondered, considering the nature of fate. I was quiet and contemplative that evening, once again very grateful to be alive.

22

Unto Dust

THE DAYS DRAGGED ON AND THE DONGALANDS showed no signs of letting up. Like the undulating Gobi desert before, they seemed to go on forever. The broken, sad ground was taking its toll on both of us. The tortured land had long since given up its ability to provide crops to the people. The ground here was sterile and exhausted. I could see remnants of where croplands once thrived. Old worn-out contour-ploughed fields etched the lonely hillsides here and there. All around, it seemed as though giant fingers had scraped massive grooves in the Earth. The erosion was seriously bad. What I really hated most was running along what appeared from afar to be relatively flat ground, only to find a huge donga suddenly appearing at my feet like a huge, gaping wound.

Unknown to me at the time, we were moving through the single largest area of soil erosion on the planet, the Loess plateau. The plateau is a massive area of compacted dust literally hundreds of feet thick. These deposits have accumulated over thousands of years as a result of howling winds and dust storms driven down from the Gobi desert in Mongolia. The dust storm we had been trapped in was a mere infant compared to the big ones in summer that sometimes blow for days.

The incredible increase in dust storms is due largely to human mismanagement. As the land is laid bare by deforestation, soil erosion and massive overgrazing, the dust storms increase in frequency and intensity. Prior to 1950 dust storms used to hit the north-west region of China approximately once every 30 years. From then till 1990 the frequency was once every 20 months. Now they blast down from Mongolia just about every year, often as far south as Beijing. I remember, during our recce trip, standing in Tiananmen Square. I could not see the far side of the famous plaza because of the sepia mist of dust that the wind had carried from hundreds of kilometres away. Many people wore face masks.

A massive 70 per cent of the plateau is already destroyed by erosion, due mainly to bad farming practices. China is among the countries most severely damaged by erosion. A staggering five billion tons of soil is lost each year and 19 per cent of the country's land area is now affected. The Loess plateau lies in the middle region of the Yellow River basin and much of the soil run-off ends up in the river, resulting in massive sediment build-ups. The sediment discharge from the Yangtze River alone exceeds the combined discharges of the two longest rivers in the world, the Amazon and Nile. The result is that China's navigable river channels have been shortened by as much as half.

Soil fertility has dropped dramatically. Apart from erosion and deser-tification, in the north-west of China the long-term use of fertilisers and pesticides has rendered about half the former cropland sterile. I would constantly point out areas of over-grazing to David, where the landscape was scarred by what resembled fish scales.

While the country's per-capita food consumption as well as its popula-tion is on the increase, its area of cropland is rapidly shrinking. In the past decade alone overgrazing, mainly by goats, in north China has brought about the desertification of approximately 15 per cent of the remaining agricultural land.

The Loess plateau is an inhospitable place and is visited only by crazy people like David and me, and occasionally scientists: some years back 16 scientists perished on the Loess plateau.

'What would scientists want to be doing among all this ancient dust?' I had asked myself.

I found the answer in the book *Six Degrees* by Mark Lynas, which gives apocalyptic scenarios for what the world would be like through each rise of a degree in average temperature.

He explains how paleo-climatologists study core samples of soil (in this case dust and sand; it can also be ice from continental glaciers, or the sea bed) and can then reconstruct climatic changes in ancient times. In 1999 a sample drawn from 30 metres down on the Loess plateau revealed soil deposited around 129,000 years ago. This was a warm period just before the onset of the last major ice age. At that time, the earth was one degree warmer than it is today. The prevailing climate was a period of severe drought with dust storms covering the entire continent.

As global temperatures continue to rise, many scientists believe that what happened then is on the cards for us in the not-too-distant future unless drastic measures are taken to prevent continued human-induced global warming. For China it translates to a massive increase in water shortages, already one of the country's most dire problems. China is also struggling to feed itself. In 1995 the world's most populous country was forced to import grain to feed its people for the first time.

As I carefully navigated my way down a particularly steep and crumbling donga, I looked down at the dark shadows below. For a moment I felt like I was walking into the abyss of hell. I pictured myself descending into a sterile, dead place. An eerie, chemical stench greeted us from below, and I felt as though David and I were going to be swallowed by the result of our species' collective sins. I thought about how our greed for self-gratification was gobbling the Earth's natural bounty and so robbing our children of a wholesome future. I thought of my son Benjamin. Maybe it was because I was very tired and angry at the physical pain I was enduring, or maybe it was because I understood all too well what was happening to the planet, but I cried going down that donga on the lonely Loess plateau.

China afforded me the opportunity to see first-hand that all environmental problems are in fact global issues. From what I saw there, and from what I have subsequently studied, I know it is my task to take the message of greater awareness for the plight of our planet to as many people as I can. We need to stand up, individually or in groups, and practise sustainable behaviour, by minimising our impact and resource use, and safeguarding irreplaceable ecosystems we rely upon for our very survival. Everything else is suicide.

Just as I had become disheartened by the Gobi desert, by this stage I'd grown all too weary of the Loess plateau. I was sick of the degraded donga-lands. I had had enough of the dead-ends, the dongas, the sand, the wind and the dust of this place of despair. The sterility of the land was squeezing my soul as if it was a sponge. I was tired, physically, mentally and spiritu-ally. I was totally *gatvol*.

But that state of mind wasn't going to help me in my quest; I had to change it or it would undo me. At least each day brought me one day closer to the fulfilment of my dream. Also the wastelands had taught me a valuable lesson: never *ever* assume that things are as you think they are, or how they should be or how you want them to be. It's something I used to do a lot, especially as a kid. I'm sure we all do. But I know now how harmful it can be.

Those hard days in the dongalands stirred up painful childhood memories. In the dozing state before sleep each night, and in the long, lonely hours of running, I realised how much I missed my family, how much I loved them and yet how little I had shown it. I knew it was something I carried over inside of me from my own childhood. I thought of my dead father and my dead brother, my only sister, my twin youngest brothers, and my sad mother. I realised how the assumptions I had made had caused me to judge others and blame them – and how lonely I had become in that bitter place. I felt that loneliness now, in this wasteland, but I could also see the gift of insight it was giving me. I wept on that barren sand in the days that followed and I learned to forgive, really forgive. Most of all I learned that I had to forgive myself for the things of my past that haunted me.

With the later knowledge of what had happened to my mother long before I was born, I thought I had forgiven her. But I still needed to go to a place deep inside myself to understand my pain in order to release myself from it. It was a long, self-examining week during which my spiritual pain overtook my physical pain. It made me see that, because I assumed I was somehow not worthy of love, I had blocked my own capacity to love.

I had blamed my mother for not loving me enough. I had blamed her for not loving my father enough. I had blamed my father for not loving his children enough. Then, when I came to understand their backgrounds, I blamed myself for blaming them. I had tied myself up in a psychological knot. And now here I was attempting maybe the hardest thing I would ever do, one of the hardest things that just about anyone would ever do. But how would I be able to reach my fullest potential if I did not fully respect myself?

And all the while, as I unravelled my emotional conundrum, I came to understand it. Then I was able to let it go, which seemed to lift my spirit, and then my body. The pain in my feet did not go away, it was something like being on laughing gas: it just didn't seem to matter as much as it had before. In my own forgiving of myself I became a wiser man. For the first time, in the loneliness of the Loess plateau, I felt the full love inside of myself for others, and in doing so I learned to truly love myself.

Now I was ready for higher ground – body, mind and spirit.

23

None so Blind

THE LANDSCAPE WAS BEGINNING TO CHANGE NOTICEABLY. The eroded gullies became fewer, the ridges more pronounced, rugged and ever less easy to navigate.

Although Garmin showed a bearing directly ahead, not only did the Wall not go that way, but the terrain blocked us by putting cliffs or steep valleys in the way. There were still areas where erosion was bad and the Wall had vanished. We would move from one lonely tower to the next, navigating our way through endless, deep gullies. Often, thinking we were on the right track, we would wind our way through a valley only to find it was a dead-end box canyon. This was terribly frustrating because it meant doubling back a few kilometres, thus trebling that distance, which started to play havoc with my recently healed mind.

These were the real foothills and, while I was relieved and even a little elated to be there, they soon proved to have their own obstacles and dangers. Here, moving past the town of Fugu, the first watchtowers built entirely of stone began to appear. New challenges presented themselves as our support team found it increasingly more difficult to track our progress along the Wall and locate us at the end of each day. We, on the other hand, had to trust them implicitly to do so. As the weather began to close in, we would grow more and more dependent on them.

We would need to leave the Wall, particularly in the high mountains, earlier in the day than we'd previously had to so we could find the campsite before dark. Although we would still average a marathon each day, a good portion of it would have to be off the actual course of the Wall. Not only was this frustrating, it meant the journey would take longer. We had not factored in the cumulative time it would take in reaching the support team each day. Then, of course, we would have to backtrack to the last Wall GPS point of the previous day. In the end, this would add a hefty 703 extra kilometres to our journey!

Day after frustrating day I just plodded on. I had learned many weeks earlier not to think the next day would be any better than the one I was in.

'Just get through today,' I repeated to myself each morning, 'you just need to get through today.'

The strain of driving and navigating was also taking its toll on the crew. At the end of a stressful day, when David and I had had a serious argument, we had to hike almost 12 kilometres from the Wall to get to the team.

When we arrived it was obvious there was tension in the camp. The Chinese contingent was sitting well apart from the Austrians, with Piou, the interpreter, vacillating between the two groups. At the end of a demanding day – which was every day – the very last thing we needed was tension in the ranks. They were there to support David and me, not compound an already stressful situation.

I called Piou to one side and asked what was going on.

'Michael and Hans refuse to drive with the rest of the team,' he said with concern. 'They say the Chinese drivers drive crazy and they will not continue in the vehicles.'

Michael was a stubborn guy. *Stur* was a word he had used often, which is Austrian for 'pig-headed'. He said he would rather walk in the mountains with Hans and meet up, as we did, at the end of the day. While I knew he was capable of it, I also knew it was a potential problem on a number of fronts – most importantly that he was the team doctor. What if he was needed? But Michael was insistent and inflexible. I was certainly in no mood for a head-bashing session and decided to leave it for a few days. There was a rest day just three days away and it would have to wait till then. On the other hand I was becoming more concerned about the Chinese team's unwillingness to split the vehicles for effective forward planning.

Setting off from camp the next morning was a blessing as tension was tangible in the crew's silence. They were like a bunch of sulking school kids with long faces. No-one made eye contact. David was also quiet. I'm sure he knew that I was getting ready to confront the problem. For me, this was not one of those situations where I could bite my tongue for anything more than a few days. The problem was serious and needed to be resolved urgently. It could jeopardise the expedition as we headed towards the high mountains; the days got shorter, temperatures plummeted and team support was paramount for success.

Once on the run I began discussing the situation with David. He felt an extra sense of responsibility, I think, because the Austrians were more his friends than mine. David defended Michael and Hans, not really admitting there was a major problem. This just angered me further. I tried rationalising the situation. Trying to talk with more logic and less emotion, I explained that if medical attention was needed, we wouldn't be able to reach Michael. I went on to say that the team had obviously become divided and that it was a serious problem. I felt it imperative that we resolve this potentially hazardous dilemma as soon as possible.

David and I argued. He said they were adults and would sort it out themselves. I wondered how, as the Austrians meandered the hills during the day, strengthening their resolve in the matter, and the Chinese reinforced their position of staying together. In my view, all that was happening was that each group was confirming what assholes the other group were. There was no-one to mediate or pull rank. I believed that David and I needed to consolidate things ourselves and issue ultimatums.

I began to lose my focus, putting unnecessary energy into trying to resolve the issues in my head. Issues that, in my opinion, would have been resolved if David had supported me in reuniting the team. David would not confront them at all. It was going to have to be up to me and I didn't like it one bit. On the third day of Michael and Hans going on their own adventure, I decided to talk to David again. The following day was a rest day and I needed to rest, knowing that things were resolved before starting out on another strenuous week. David was my friend and partner in this thing and I expected his support. We needed to stand united and be seen to do so.

I explained my view in detail, expressing both my logical and emotional standpoints. I felt he listened well, then asked what I proposed. I suggested we have a round-table discussion that evening with all team members present, allowing each individual to express their view. This would take great skill from Piou, as his accurate interpretation would be vital. David and I would mediate, and I impressed on him the importance of us standing as one. If a solution was not reached and agreed to by all parties, David and I would spend time together on rest day and make a joint decision and then act on it. David was in agreement with my proposal. I admired his maturity, as I knew it might be harder for him than me, not only because the Austrians were essentially his friends, but also because he is much less of a confrontational person than I am.

At dinner that night, sitting around the table like Knights of the Round Table, I called a meeting and laid out the problem. Hans was more flexible and open to discussion than Michael. Michael felt that, as he was not being paid, he was entitled to a bit of a holiday. He did not want to be in a vehicle most of the day and simply refused to comply with our request. He said if I didn't like it, he would just go home. The situation became heated and I felt it better to leave the discussion at that point and discuss it further with David the next day. We didn't bring up the issue of the Chinese team splitting the vehicles, as it would have just added fuel to the fire.

After more tension between David and me, we finally agreed that Michael would be given an ultimatum: shape up or ship out. If he would not act in the best interests of the expedition, he would be driven to the nearest rail station where he would be dropped off and left to his own affairs. In a sense, he had already threatened us with that option. The ultimatum was never delivered; it proved unnecessary after something remarkable happened.

Michael was sitting on a step on the dusty roadside playing his harmonica. A blind boy moved towards Michael, intrigued by the sound, his stick tapping the ground until he stood next to the source of the sound. The Austrian man reached out his hand and gently held the Chinese boy's arm, the boy resting his other hand on Michael. I was sitting some distance away and was deeply moved as I watched tears slowly run down the *stur* man's cheeks. It was a side to him I had not seen, or expected. I just watched in silence.

That evening Michael earned my deepest respect and I believe the respect of the entire crew. Earlier that day Hans had helped break the ice by talking alone with Michael. Dinner started out strained, with a noticeable chill in the room. Michael quietly asked if he could say something and we nodded. He stood up and, in his best English, apologised to the rest of us. It must have been a very difficult thing to do, because he had to pause while Piou interpreted. He apologised for having put himself first, for letting his ego dominate his emotions and for potentially jeopardising the expedition. I was taken aback. His courage, humility and maturity was a catalyst that united the team and bonded us like never before. I admire him and to this day I am proud to call him my friend.

A team is as strong as its weakest link, so the saying goes. To be an asset it is vital, firstly, to subscribe to the overall goal of the team and, secondly, to understand the unique contribution you bring to the team. You are either an asset or a liability – there is no middle ground; if you are not an asset, you are a liability. In nature, if you are a liability you are taken out of the team either by being rejected or killed. Suddenly, the members of our team in China understood the valuable asset they each were. Each individual felt valued and appreciated. We realised the competition was the Wall and the winter: there was no need to compete against each other.

THE MOUNTAINS

Kingdom between Heaven and Hell

大山
—
天
堂
與
地
獄
之
間
的
領
域

24

Solitude

MOUNTAINS ARE SPECIAL PLACES FOR ME. There is a silence there that is different to the desert, or anywhere else. Mountains hold mystery and wonder in their crags and a certain peace is found on the summits. I have always found my soul food in the high places. Living in Cape Town, in the shadow of Table Mountain, I could always look up at the majesty and silence of its heights. There was a peace there that was missing in the hustle and bustle of urban living.

Once, after an argument with my Dad about religion, he came and sat at the foot of my bed and spoke to me about God and the mountain.

'You see,' he began, 'the mountain is a little like God. We live down here and look up at the mountain in awe. It is a big thing and often we are scared of her. She stands out amongst the suburbs that surround her, reminding us of our innocence, of where we came from, and we are drawn to her constantly,' he said passionately.

'We go to her and try to discover her in a multitude of ways. Some people walk the contour path around her lower slopes, and they learn plenty from what they feel, smell and see. They may spend most weekends exploring her different sides over many years. Other more adventurous folk take ropes, harnesses and other climbing gear and carefully scale great, seemingly impenetrable cliffs, sometimes finding rest in the strangest high places as they gaze down at the humming city below,' he continued.

'No one path is the only path to the summit. Some parents want to show their children the view from the top, but they are often too young to walk or climb. So mom and dad save their money in the suburbs until they can pay for a ride to the top in the cable car,' he went on, his hand on my ankle, rubbing it to emphasise the point.

'You see,' he said, 'there is no right path to the top. In fact, it is only when you are at the top, at the very highest point, that you can honestly look all around you and truly understand why each person has chosen their particular path.'

I finally got it and all the while my dad continued caressing my ankle, occasionally squeezing it to emphasise another point.

'You see,' he said again, 'when you can see all around you from the top of the mountain; you understand why people climb the mountain or simply meander along her many paths, because they come from different places with different views of the same mountain. No-one is right and no-one is wrong. You can be with God, at the top of the climb, at the highest point, or walking along a footpath around the slopes. And when you feel God like that, you will understand that there is no judgement,' my dad concluded, as though somehow trying to convince himself.

I struggled with that then and still do now at times.

'No judgement,' I often say to myself when I catch myself casting aspersions on someone, or someone's point of view. In my heart, I know that it's the way it should be. Who am I to judge one religion while favouring another? Are we not all climbing the same mountain? Perhaps that's why I am with my own personal god when I am in raw nature.

Everything we know, everything we are taught, comes from nature. It is when I stop listening to the lessons around me and stop appreciating the gifts I have been given, that I begin to lose my sense of spirit. When we turn our backs on nature, I believe we turn our backs on our personal god.

Many people still do not believe that the Earth is a living entity: my question to them is, then how come it can die, as it is starting to do right now? Now, running carefully, often walking over a badly eroded landscape, I thought of Beaverlac and the sheer beauty and wildness of the mountains and rivers that wind through my special place. I had been going to that nature-lovers' retreat in the Grootwinterhoek mountains for close on 35 years. I used to hitchhike to the place when I was still a youngster. I now own a cabin there, which I built on exactly the same spot where I used to pitch my tent as a teenager. The tall trees that give me shade there in summer were once saplings in black plastic bags that I had bought from a nursery and lovingly planted.

As I ran and walked over the barren, gullied dongalands, I thought of the Cape weaver birds in the trees next to my cabin. The males would be building nests now, weaving their incredible structures while hanging upside down and expertly threading the long strips of grass with their beaks, all the while making shrill chattering sounds proclaiming their territories. Then, when completed, they would hang from the opening, fluffing their bright yellow chests and flapping their wings, trying to attract a mate, screeching as loudly as possible. If he was lucky, the duller female would enter the nest, inspect it thoroughly and move in first time. If, however, his labours did not meet her perfectionist standards she'd move off to another suitor, but not before viciously demolishing the entire structure while the poor male looked on dejected. I smiled as I ran, missing their loud yellow brightness here in the dull, bland, endless badlands of the great central Asian steppe.

Most years at Beaverlac I would hike up to a high basin about six kilometres from the campsite. The views of the folded mountains all around me, with no sign of any human habitation anywhere, are awesome and really do take your breath away. Sitting on my familiar cliff ledge, I would peer down the steep cliffs at the pristine Dwars River below as it snaked its way between rock walls and rough boulder banks. Then, after taking it all in, I would leave the trail behind me and scramble down the kilometre or so of steep, fynbos-covered ground to the sanctuary of the wild valley below.

My ritual would always be the same: stripping naked, I would bury my clothes in the coarse white river sand and place a cairn of rocks on top. Hiking upriver, I'd swim two long pools flanked by steep, smooth rock walls. Then, after about another kilometre, I would arrive at my special place – a small, white sand beach with a clear golden-brown pool. This would be my home for the following three nights and nature would provide for all my needs.

The Bushmen in the Kalahari desert had taught me the art of making fire with sticks and the Shangaan trackers in the Kruger National Park had also. The trick was to have a hard boring stick and a softer wood plate for the base, and to make sure the boring stick was as straight as possible. Making a small hole in the softer piece of wood with a sharp stone, I then cut two narrow grooves down either side of the hole. Making sure the harder boring stick fitted comfortably into the hole, sitting down, I braced the soft-wood plate with my feet. Beneath it was a ball of very fine, fluffy tinder. I usually used a mixture of fine grasses and dry dassie scat, which I crushed and rolled into a loose, fist-size ball.

Placing my hands at the top of the straight stick, I rubbed them vigorously together, backwards and forwards, keeping downwards pressure on the hole, moving my hands down the stick. When I reached the base I needed to quickly move to the top and repeat the movement, over and over and over. When friction began to turn to fire, fine, minute coals would fall down the grooves onto the tinder below and smoke would begin drifting up. When there was enough smoke rising from the tinder ball, I would quickly but carefully pick it up and blow gently until a flame appeared. That small flame would signal the start of my hearth, and would remain alight until extinguished four days later. It was the ritualistic start of my 'alone time'.

I would keep myself busy for the remainder of my first day and the first few hours of darkness plaiting fishing line and cord from the palmiet reeds along the river bank, splicing hooks from animal bones or crab pincers and making and setting traps. The traps were not all that effective as the animals along the river banks were predominantly small and agile, such as grey mongoose, water mongoose and spotted genets. The much larger Cape clawless otter, baboon, caracal and leopard were not exactly what I intended eating! Easiest of the land animals to catch was the dassie, or rock hyrax. Although only the size of a fat rabbit, its closest relative is, in fact, the African elephant.

But 'easy' is a relative word. Catching a dassie required me to be incredibly patient because they dart into rock crevices when approached. Spotting an area where they sunned themselves, I would select a specific point, climb to a higher position, carefully straddle the narrow groove where they lived, my butt on a log or wedged rock, a foot on either side of the groove and a heavy rock resting on my thighs. Sitting still and quiet with a numb bum for 20 minutes or so is no easy task. When the animals think the threat is over, they move out into the sun again.

I always let at least two move out first to increase my chances of success. With a clear visual between my legs, I would simply part them and let the rock drop the metre or two onto the unfortunate animal below. Fast and effective in execution, but often very time consuming in the 'stalking'. In the many years I have spent in the Dwars valley, I have not caught more than half a dozen of the animals. Dassie is a fatty meat but seriously tasty when slow-cooked over coals. If I caught one, it was enough food for my entire time alone.

Much easier to catch were the brown river crabs, also favoured by the otters. Because they are small, I would need to catch at least 10 of them to make a decent meal. I would cut them in two with a sharp stone and lay them on coals. Occasionally, using a frog as bait, I would catch a Clanwilliam yellowfish. These are protected fish as their populations have been decimated by the alien bass that were introduced into the Oliphants River system for sport-fishing. Fortunately, the bass have not been able to infest the Dwars River because there are two waterfalls too high for the bass to climb. The upper reaches of the river teem with small yellowfish and I was in no way damaging the ecological balance. If anything I was being a part of it – the apex cave-man predator.

The summer sun would reach my section of the river for only about six hours a day, which was more than enough because the temperatures in the height of summer would peak in the low 40s. On one special occasion, I had been lying in the water and had moved out onto a rock, where I was sunning myself like a crag lizard. Getting too hot, I had moved further across the rock into the dappled shade. The rock lay angled, sloping gently down to the water like a slipway. I suddenly noticed a large shape moving in the shade of a kliphout tree on the opposite bank. Lying motionless, I watched with great curiosity.

Initially, I thought it was a baboon. The animal stopped in the shadow. I could see nothing but sensed it was there. Then, moving out onto a long, knife-edged rock into full sunlight, there appeared the most beautiful male leopard I had ever seen. Not more than 20 metres away, with only the water separating us, he was totally unaware of me. He reached the water's edge, looked up and down the length of the pool and then directly at me. I could see his mouth half open, gently panting. I hardly breathed and didn't even blink. He crouched down and leisurely drank the cool water. After pausing to look up for a moment, as though at me again, he casually continued drinking.

I cannot say how long he drank for, it seemed a few minutes but those moments were priceless. As he stood up from his crouched position, he turned like a tight-rope walker on the thin edge of rock. Pausing, he looked over his shoulder at the water, or was it at me? With his mouth still hanging half open, showing his magnificent white canines, he flicked the end of his tail a few times before stealthily vanishing into the shadows. It was one of the most special moments nature has ever bestowed on me and one I will cherish always.

Of the 10 species of large cat found in Africa, the leopard (*Panthera pardus*) and the caracal (*Felis caracal*) are, without doubt, the two most versatile: both occur in these mountains. They are highly adaptive, highly secretive and both are capable of covering huge areas to mark and protect their territories. The leopards found in the Western Cape are often called

Cape mountain leopards, but, although considerably smaller than their northern savanna relatives and rarely weighing more than 40 kilograms, they are not in fact a separate species. Unlike leopards found in the bushveld regions, the Cape leopards have no other big predator competition such as hyenas or lions. They are opportunistic, eating anything from beetles and mice to dassies and baboons, and occasionally livestock, predominantly sheep. Scats show dassies to be their main diet in the Cape.

Their territories are vast, spanning sometimes more than 1,000 kilometres and usually incorporating high mountains. The combination of large mountainous territories, no serious predator competition and relatively small prey, has caused them to have evolved into lighter, more endurance athlete-type animals. Their relatives in the northern savanna regions, who occupy smaller territories and regularly have to haul large carcasses into trees to avoid having their prey stolen by hyenas or lions, are naturally heavier and stronger, often weighing twice as much as their Cape cousins.

I have often seen spoor and scats of leopards around Beaverlac but, apart from animals trapped for relocation, I have seen only that one beautiful male on that hot day drinking from the cool Dwars water.

At night I kept the fire going, with just one large flickering log. Before turning in I would spread the now substantial bed of coals in a pit about a metre by half a metre and cover the bed of coals with a thick layer of the dry river sand. My bed would keep me warm all night.

Lying naked, nestled half-buried in the sand, the sounds of running water close by, the occasional barking of baboons somewhere in the night and the shimmering canopy of billions of stars, the contrasting coal-black cliffs would hold the river and me in their comforting rocky arms. In those moments I would feel connected to nature in the most intensely primal way. I could sense how all atoms and molecules that made up this world – including me, each grain of sand, even the billions of stars above and everything in this universe – were made of the same elements.

When the time came to leave the mountain sanctuary I would shake the sand from my clothes and put them on with a feeling of inexplicable sadness. Sad that I needed to be clothed and sad to leave the spiritual peace I had absorbed in this sacred place.

After the hard climb to the crest of the valley's ridge, I always stopped and sat for a few minutes on my cliff ledge and said a silent farewell to the magic place below that had given me so much in such a short time. It felt as though an important connection was being severed. Leaving my valley, I would begin to yearn for that feeling of connectedness to nature that could not be gained in the seemingly safe world we humans have created for ourselves.

As I turned my back, a haunting sadness lingered with me as I began the six kilometre walk down and back to my cabin. The irregular track was flanked by hundreds of species of proteas, ericas and restios and occasionally a pair of Verreaux's eagles would dance silent patterns between the rocks and the pale blue sky. I derived a comfort from them on the walk. I knew my cabin would just be a gentle interlude for a few days before going back to the so-called 'real world'. There was nothing more real than where I had been.

As I ran through the gutted, eroded route along China's Great Wall, I remembered how it was usually the simple things that thrilled me the most. Sitting on my cabin's wooden deck with my dogs lying sleeping in the long grass close by, the fire alight in the braai pit and the soft wind in the high branches, I would sip my whisky as I watched the light fade on the distant Koue Bokkeveld mountains. I missed that tranquillity now, as I puffed my way out of yet another confounded gully in the all too real madness of this crazy running challenge.

25

Journey of 10,000 Li

THE DAYS GREW COLDER STILL as the land rose up before us, now very real and high. The daily morning temperatures were between −10 and −15 °C and – even though I had not been able to get out of the flatlands fast enough – I hated this new cold element I had to deal with. You've probably realised by now that I love mountains, but still give me heat over cold any day. And we were not yet into the highest of them. The cold was not something I could train for in South Africa. Even the wet Cape Town winter training runs on Table Mountain could not have prepared me for this.

Getting out of my sleeping bag in the dark was the worst of it. I was reading the book *Mind Over Matter* by the great modern explorer, Ranulph Fiennes. It is the story of his incredible crossing of the Antarctic on foot. Fiennes did the journey with his friend, Dr Mike Stroud, unassisted, in 100 days. They experienced temperatures in the minus 40s ... and I thought I had it bad! It motivated me tremendously as I read about their adventure in my tent at night before sleeping.

'One day at a time; that's how they did it and that's how I am doing it,' my mantra echoed in my head.

Seeing the high mountain ridges looming in the distance, the feeling of excitement and tension balled in my gut. I knew I had grown consistently stronger and was ready for the new challenge. The next day we would be there, on one of those distant peaks. I laid out the extra kit I would need for the weeks still to come: bigger pack, full static line rope, harness, extra medical supplies, extra food, sleeping bag. The days were going to become even slower with little, if any, running. They were shorter too, as winter now set in. Leaves blew across the ground like lonely, lost dancers and even the sallow sun looked cold as it hovered hesitantly on the horizon. I slept well that night, deeply, with no dreams I could remember.

The cold morning came too soon. Frost was on the ground and my tent creaked as the ice cracked and fell while I dressed. It was −16 °C as I crunched my way up the gorge towards the Wall, high in the dark grey dawn above me. The barren ground in the stunned forest on the steep slopes was slippery underfoot and the going really slow. There were horrible thorn bushes that broke off and stuck to me like parasites. My gloves looked like black hedgehogs. Once the 2 cm-long spike had attached itself, the end split and opened, allowing an even sharper needle-like barb to penetrate through my glove, or any other part of clothing it had latched on to. Once it reached my skin, it felt like a sharp pin prick and forced me to get my outer mitts off and spend good minutes pulling the confounded things out one at a time with my teeth. Pull, spit, pull, spit. Fortunately these little devils grew only in the gullies on the lower slopes.

As I scrambled onto the Wall, the horizon boasted a beautiful sunrise. The view was breathtaking and I was in awe of the magnificence of the Earth as I began a steep ascent of hundreds of narrow steps. 'Dangerous' is an understatement: the steps up the gradients were so narrow I had to place my feet sideways, one above the other. There was light snow, and one slip, one misplaced foot, would end in a painful death. The gradients were often near-vertical – how they were built was beyond me.

The line of the Wall generally follows the highest ridges and points of the steep mountains. Often the cliffs are so steep on either side of the ridge line that the spine is like a knife edge. Yet they built a defensive line along these impenetrable skylines in an endless snaking dragon, all the way from the Gobi desert in Central Asia to the Bo Sea, a large scallop-bite in the Yellow Sea. Occasionally the Wall would move off the ridge line and, for reasons unknown, would wind down a slope, almost to the valley bottom, then curve back up to the high ridges again. Most of the Wall along here is from the Ming dynasty.

The name of the Great Wall comes from traditional Chinese, *Wanli Chancheng*, meaning 'the ten thousand li Wall'. A *li* is a Chinese mile and is about one third of an English mile. The construction of the Wall began as far back as the 8th century BC. It is certainly not the oldest building of the ancient world, but it has been constantly under construction or repair for almost 3,000 years; this cannot be said of any other building in the world. The greatest periods of construction were during the Qin, Han, Jin and Ming dynasties. The work on the Wall under the Qin emperor extended it to over 10,000 li, hence 'the ten thousand li Wall'.

The Ming was the last dynasty to undertake large-scale work on the Wall (until 1644 when Qing nomads from Manchuria ousted the Ming emperor in Beijing). They broke down, reconstructed and built new sections as a double defensive line, an estimated 7,300 kilometres of it in total. Our journey of the Wall was along the most recognised continuous line of the Great Wall, without all the side detours. This is the Sleeping Dragon and we were following its spine, an estimated 3,500 kilometres from Jiayuguan to Shanhaiguan. However, if you were to take all the walls built inside of China, the double walls and many spurs built to trap the Mongol invaders, add these to the old Han Wall and those remnants from other dynasties, the total length of defensive lines would be something more than a staggering 30,000 kilometres!

Our journey, with all its detours and double-backs, measured just over 4,200 kilometres, or – in the notation of Mao's Long March – four million two hundred thousand steps.

26

The Great Forgetting

I HAD RUN, WALKED AND SOMETIMES CRAWLED for something like 2,500 kilometres. Now I was also climbing. There had been some light snow falls in the mountains where we were now ensconced and white drifts lay all about us, as well as etching prominent lines and features. The parapets and steps of the Wall often had little wads of snow on them.

Following the magnificent Wall for most of the day, I stopped at a watchtower. One side had broken away and crumbled to the valley far below. Looking at the construction of the barrel vault, I was truly impressed. The keystone at the high point of the arched doorway was missing, but the rest of the arch somehow remained intact. Moving upwards on the ridge-hugging Wall I came to another tower, only this time the arch on the far side did not lead back onto the Wall: the ground had vanished and all that was left was a gaping chasm. Peering over, as the wind clawed at my head, I looked down a crumbled cliff falling away. It was time for ropes.

I hauled out the 50-metre static line, set up an anchor point, put on my harness and prepared to abseil. I went first so I could belay David from below. I was impressed by how far he had come since I had first abseiled with him in training back home. He was still frightened of high places but calmly went about what needed to be done. We had done this before while adventure racing back in South Africa. It would be a multi-pitch abseil, as the route down was a good 200 metres.

Pulling the rope through the final anchor, coiling it and packing it, we began the long climb back up to the Wall on the other side of the chasm. Thorny scrub grabbed at my legs and tore small holes in my clothing, as if trying to stop me. Back on the Wall again, I chatted with David about fear. I didn't have a fear of heights, spiders, the dark or any of the conventional fears. My fear was of loss.

I shared with him how I had lost my business and gone insolvent back in 1984. It had felt as though I had been stripped naked as my 'treasures' were taken from me, one thing at a time. My car was repossessed, furniture and sound system removed, they even took my bicycle. I could get no credit for 10 years and had to move my Dad – who had been living with me since he'd had a stroke – into an old-age home because I lost my home too. I felt incredibly insecure. So much so that I even lost my fiancée. I felt I was worth nothing. And that was precisely the lesson I needed to learn, because what I had become before my insolvency was a giant ego-tripping wanker.

At the time I thought that because I stayed in a cool home, drove a cool car and had all the fancy material trappings of a successful yuppie, I had arrived somewhere special. I was the main kid on the block. But, in reality, I had become trapped. My soul had stopped growing and I had lost my true identity. I was out to impress anyone who would listen to me, but with a false image, as I had forgotten my real nature. I had become a victim of consumption and greed that is a typical aspiration of many people in the urbanised world. I now call this period 'the great forgetting'. The forgetting of what's really important. Forgetting one's soul for instant gratification. Forgetting what's real for the sake of appeasing the ego.

When I was 25 I started a small advertising agency with a friend. We had a great concept linked to a total lack of business sense. In reality, being a cocky young co-owner of an ad agency was a cool image. But that's all it was, an image. I believed my idea was so good that all the debt I was piling up was just a series of stepping stones to the big bank vault on the other side. When I couldn't pay my bills on time, and the letters of demand started arriving, the stress picked up and the partying slowed to a stop. I couldn't sleep at night as I thought of ways to get out of the hole I had dug. I put on a false smile to my mates and pretended that business was just great. All the time my ego was getting in the way and pride was eating at my gut like a cancer.

Then one day the sheriff of the court knocked on my door and delivered the first judgement against me. And then the next, and the next. I thought my life was falling apart. I was too frightened to go and see my debtors to try and make some arrangement, and instead hid away like a coward. Whenever a car pulled up outside my place, my stomach knotted. When the phone rang I hesitated before answering. I remember thinking, 'How could this be happening to me?' and trying to find blame in everyone and everything else, but never in myself.

Finally the court order was handed down. I was insolvent.

'I have nothing,' I kept saying to myself, 'I have nothing.' I felt like a total failure.

When I moved Dad to the old-age home I had to ask my aunt to assist him financially. I couldn't even look after my frail father. I promised to visit him often. One day I called and said I would see him the next day. Something else came up and I never went. He died that night. Seeing him lying so still in his bed the next morning – his hands, one on top of the other across his heart – caused such a sadness to well up inside me I thought I could die also, but I never cried. Instead of falling apart, I somehow took control. I knew my sister was on her way and I didn't want her last memory of her father to be what I was looking at. He hadn't shaved for about a week; also his hair was dishevelled and hadn't been brushed for a while. I shaved him and combed his hair – and then I quietly cried. I truly felt that I had lost everything. I remember thinking how heavy the emptiness was.

In hindsight I came to realise that what had happened was that I had been given an unasked for but life-saving hand. It pulled me out of my self-destructive groove, helping me to rediscover my way in life and redefine my values. Before my insolvency I had fallen into the trap of 'the next big fix'.

This period of change and crisis was the first important turning point in my life. My lost connection to nature returned. I moved to the beautiful freedom of nearly two hectares of land at Appleton Camp on top of Signal Hill, an old scout camp that had been left to slowly decline. In return for a long lease from the scouting association I fixed it up. Beyond my neat cottage and my own garden is the wild fynbos of what is now part of the Table Mountain National Park.

It took the shock of being laid bare of possessions for me to let go of greed and stop only taking without giving in return. It was as though I had entered into a rehab programme from the drug of consumerism. Most importantly, I took a decision to follow my passion and not money. Ironically, as a consequence, money has followed me. It was during this period in my life that I first truly understood what a gift giving can be. I wanted to be an asset to the world and chose to begin a deeper journey, to discover just what it is I really have to give.

I can now see that finding and acknowledging my place and my purpose has singularly been the greatest gift I have ever received. The second was discovering the unconditional love in the birth of my son Benjamin. I also know now that being genuinely fulfilled is a discovery that seemingly not many people make, because they usually keep looking in the wrong places.

As the writer in *The Sacred Balance* by David Suzuki, Paul Wachtel, once put it: '*Having more and newer things each year has become not just something we want, but something we need. The idea of more, of ever-increasing wealth, has become the centre of our identity and our security, and we are caught up by it like the addict by his drugs.*'

The 'great forgetting' returns – that hollow point in the solar plexus, that emptiness of something that's missing. Rather than explore what that is, most people just go out and buy something, or take something. They try to fill the emptiness with 'things' because they have forgotten the connection they once had with nature.

China is a case in point: while developing economically at an unprecedented speed, they are aspiring to reach First World levels and, like other countries in a similar arch of development, they are raping the Earth to make it happen. Every First World or 'developed' nation has already raped its natural resources – and often those of poorer countries too – to get where it is. But at least the Chinese, alone in the world, are addressing the even more serious threat to global health, that of human overpopulation.

In this economic and industrial development we seem to be moving away from our spiritual connection to nature, which is also a free resource, to surrounding ourselves with ego-satisfying goods, which provide only fleeting, and usually false, earthly satisfaction.

'*Money never made a man happy yet, nor will it. There is nothing in its nature to produce happiness. The more a man has, the more he wants. Instead of filling a vacuum, it makes one,*' said that wise old kite flier, Benjamin Franklin.

I do not see money as bad, but what I do see as bad is how we have made it a substitute for our spiritual connection with the natural world. My own insolvency provided me with a new view of things. When I look back on my life I see that nothing in it has been coincidence. Everything has had its reason, everything has had a purpose. It's only when I have tried to push against the current that I have come close to drowning. There has always been a path in front of me as clear as day. Whenever I forget that and start to feel lost or disillusioned, all I have to do is sit quietly in the wilderness and the connection returns. Or climb a mountain, paddle on the ocean, or go for a run.

For most of us our two greatest fears are fear of rejection (why people cannot stand in front of a crowd and give a speech) and the fear of loss (which makes us cling to things) – loss of a loved one, a home, a business or one's own life. When I lost my business I felt I had lost the foundations of my life. But that type of security, I discovered, can be easily replaced. When we lose a person we love we lose a part of our identity and it feels that part of us has died. It is our human connectedness that feels severed and this cannot be easily replaced. Likewise our connection to nature, even though its loss might not feel as huge as the loss of a loved one at the time. This is another 'great forgetting' because for a while everything seems to be okay. But my truth is that we need to reconnect to nature if we want to truly be rich.

When I work with children, which is a major part of what I do with my life now, they understand intuitively the lessons of nature. When I work with adults I ask that they try to think like children. Those who do also get in touch with the spirit of nature. And when they do, they honour themselves in their connection and move on with a greater purpose.

Maria Montessori, a teacher whom I have come to admire greatly, put it this way: 'The stars, Earth, stones, life of all kinds, form a whole in relation to each other. No matter what we touch, an atom or a cell, we cannot explain it without knowledge of the universe. The laws governing the universe can be made interesting and wonderful to children, more interesting than things in themselves, and they begin to ask: What am I? What is the task of humanity in this wonderful universe?'

27

The Knife's Edge

THE MOUNTAINS WERE STEEP and the going was slow. My pack weighed around 17 kilos and an icy wind blew as we followed the Wall. We had moved down a broad valley to what could have been an old fortress, but was now a tiny rural village inhabited by peasant subsistence farmers. We stopped in a wind shelter of old crumbled Wall and I put my legs up as I ate lunch. Lying back I noticed fast, sickle-shaped clouds moving above the ridge in our line of travel. Lenticular clouds are a sign of impending bad weather, usually coming in rapidly, so we knew something was brewing in the heavens. We still had 15 kilometres to cover and I had no idea of the terrain ahead. With the wind-chill factor, it was at least −20°C and looking bleak. I suggested we cut lunch short and move. David agreed.

By the time we had covered two kilometres and had reached the ridge line of the Wall, the fast-moving cloud had caught us. I guessed the wind speed at around 40 kilometres an hour. Having lived in Cape Town, with its characteristic howling summer southeaster winds, I knew I was pretty accurate. It was gusting hard, throwing up powder snow, and visibility was no more than 10 metres. The bandana that covered my nose and mouth was frozen from the wetness caused by heavy breathing. We were up at over 3,000 metres and relied on the Wall as our only guide. The Wall here was really broken and treacherous and I used my poles to feel the ground ahead to ensure I made solid foot placements. This was not a place to break an ankle. The wind swirled around us, enveloping us in cold white dust as we moved forward at a snail's pace.

On flat ground, with a light pack, a person walks a kilometre in around 12 minutes. We were covering 200 metres in the same time! With four layers of upper-body gear and three around my legs, I couldn't believe how cold I was. My state-of-the-art Adidas kit was high-tech fabric and designed for this environment; but it was the wind-chill that was getting to me. You can't stay in the watchtowers; it's worse than outside because the wind gets sucked through them and spirals around. I shouted to David, who was barely visible, that we needed to get off the mountain. Easier said than done. We needed to find a do-able escape route, one that had been travelled by shepherds, as opting to go down the side would be tantamount to falling off a cliff.

My concentration was intense as I watched my feet and tried looking for a way down; visibility was now about five metres. Head lamps were useless up there because the beam just reflected off the clouds and spindrift. I thought, in trying to hear David's shouting, that he wasn't making any sense. Later, he said he had thought the same of me. Hypothermia was on the cards. My chattering had subsided and I started feeling way too okay for the situation.

'Do the count, do the count,' I screamed at David. 'I'll start – one thousand, two thousand, three thousand ...,' all the way to 10, I yelled out aloud.

Then David did the same. It was one of our survival plans, to check each other's sanity in case of hypothermia. When you get hypothermia, one of the symptoms is feeling great when you are, in fact, on the way out. Another is speaking gobbledygook. At one point I got to around seven and forgot where I was in my count. David said he had experienced the same. We really needed to get off the mountain fast and, more importantly, out of the wind, and warm up.

Then I saw it – a narrow scramble of a path on my left. It was headed in the right direction, taking us into the lee of the wind. It didn't mean we were safe yet, I knew that. We were both cold, exhausted and speaking rubbish.

'Keep counting,' shouted David.

It kept us connected and focused.

The path got beyond steep. It was too dangerous. I guessed it had been made by goats and not shepherds! I took the rope out at a point and belayed David down. At another section of cliff we had to remove our gloves for better grip to avoid slipping. After only a minute or so I couldn't feel anything with my hands and had to put my gloves back on. David found an overhang out of the wind.

'Here,' he shouted, 'there's cover here.'

We squeezed into the small overhang.

'Bivvy bags,' I shouted back, 'we have to get warm or it's over.'

I lay in my bivvy bag in silence, my mouth close to the small breathing hole. My head was spinning all over the show. I drifted from being very lucid to a dream-like weightlessness. I felt almost high. Was I going to die here, I wondered, in a half daze?

'I'm spared from the dust storm, spared from the mud, just to end up dying here on this stupid mountain,' I berated myself.

'No way!' I muttered.

Panic threatens to consume you and it can all too easily undo you. You have to use willpower to fight it back, then logic: 'When I get warm I will be able to get things together. Then I'll just take it 10 metres at a time. It's downhill and the wind will be less fierce. I am *not* going to die here, that's it,' I scolded myself.

We lay there for at least an hour, retaining some heat in our bivvy bags and slowly getting our internal temperature gauges up. David and I hardly spoke, each of us wrapped in our own thoughts. In that long hour I thought of Ben.

'How could I have been so selfish?' I asked myself for the umpteenth time on the journey.

The light was fading fast; we needed to move.

'How're you feeling?' I asked.

'Warmer. You?' came the reply.

'I'm good, I think! How's your head space?' I asked with a slight chuckle.

'No, cool. But we should move, we're losing light and there's no way I want to stay out here tonight,' replied David.

I was in full agreement.

We stuffed our luminous yellow bags into our packs and started the slow descent. It was a steep slope with lots of loose rocks and we couldn't see far ahead, so we used the rope for safety. I tied it off and David would scramble down to a safe point. Sometimes I couldn't see or hear him in the swirling cloud, so I would feel for slack in the rope before following. The rope was 50 metres but we couldn't do more than about 20 metres at a time because I had to feed it through an anchor above me and then climb down to where David was. I usually found a smoothish rock to loop the rope around, but I also had a pile of Prusik cords that Michael had given me. If I couldn't find an anchor that allowed for a smooth pull-through, I would undo the Prusik cords and join them with double-fisherman's knots. The only problem with that was we'd have to leave them attached at the anchor point. Not knowing how many more anchors we needed meant trying to use as few Prusik cords as possible.

As I watched the altitude drop on Garmin, I felt progressively safer and better. Finally we climbed below the cloud and I felt a lot happier. It was almost dark by then and I had no idea where we were. There was no cell signal so we hadn't received an SMS with camp co-ordinates from the support crew. Following the Wall we would have eventually picked up a signal, but we had left the Wall and were headed to who knew where. We reached a valley and found a dry river bed with weathered boulders, which we followed. We moved in silence as the valley widened, our head lights bobbing up and down like drunk fire flies. Rounding a corner, we saw faint lights in the distance.

'Looks like a village,' David said.

'At last,' I sighed. Although we still had a few kilometres to go, I immediately felt lighter somehow.

Again, I was sincerely grateful for my life. I was walking a few metres ahead of David. I stopped and turned to him.

'Come here,' I said, with arms outstretched.

'What now?' he asked and pulled up.

I hugged him hard. We both had watery eyes.

'That's also from Ben,' I said.

Two days earlier my son had sent me an SMS. He ended his message with 'and give David a hug from me'. I hadn't of course; it wasn't the macho thing to do. When your ego is put on the back-burner and your life is laid on the line, you can see very clearly what's important. Your priorities fall into order and you get to understand and appreciate what is real and what holds meaning for you. Most often it's the simple things that we otherwise take for granted.

When we reached the village we were able to pick up signal and sent our co-ordinates to the team, where they finally came to collect us. It was late and I was utterly exhausted. After a warm Lilly stew I crawled into my tent, touched Benjamin's stone and fell asleep almost instantly.

28

Confucius Says

THE FOLLOWING DAY BROKE TO BLUE SKIES and no wind. It was a different world, although snow coated the higher ground. Lunga took us to where they had waited for us the night before. There was an easy access of only two kilometres to the Wall, but we had to backtrack five more kilometres to get to where we had left it the day before. Looking down where we had descended, I wondered if I would have attempted it if I had seen it in clear light. It was suicidally steep and an awfully long way down.

After 20 kilometres of hectic ups and downs that morning, I sat outside a watchtower, my back against the cold stone, and let the sun warm me. Although it was −7 °C, there was no wind and my black windbreaker and leggings absorbed the warmth. It felt so good I didn't want to move on. I felt a gravitational pull anchoring me to the Wall. Before getting on with the day, we studied our dodgy A4 map. I could see a rail line running first through the Wall and then, curving back, it appeared to run right on top of it!

'See what I mean about inaccurate maps,' I said to David. 'I mean, how does a rail line go along the Wall, and especially up and down along it!'

We both laughed at the obvious mistake the cartographers had made.

We had moved no more than two kilometres from lunch when David pointed out a long railway bridge spanning a wide gorge to the left of the Wall. It seemed to head towards the Wall and then disappear behind a buttress. The Wall was, as per pretty much normal, very broken and fragmented and seemed to be getting worse. Heading down a steep incline, it just broke away and vanished. There wasn't even a sign of the missing rocks anywhere.

'Where the heck did it go?' I asked rhetorically.

'Maybe it wasn't built, maybe it's a gap for ambushes,' replied David.

'Confucius says!' we said simultaneously. It had become a regular phrase between us. There were so many incidents for which we couldn't find any logical explanation, so we coined the Confucius phrase.

Looking across the valley with my binoculars, there was no sign of Wall anywhere. On a distant peak, which I guessed to be about 10 kilometres away, was a watchtower. We slipped and slid down the slope to the valley floor, where we picked up a well-trodden path heading around the buttress. Following it was easy and a pleasure as it was the first bit of flat terrain we'd traversed in days. We decided to run to make up time. As we came around the bend, spanning the valley high above us there was another railway bridge. It was at least a kilometre long and didn't go around the mountain as we had thought – it went right into it in the direction of the distant tower. The map was right, except it didn't go on top of the Wall, it went pretty much underneath it along the same line as the Wall but right through the mountains. I remembered William telling us of the long train tunnels in China. These trains were for moving vast quantities of coal from the Shanxi province in the north-west to the big cities on the coast.

After a lengthy discussion and a re-look at the map, we decided to climb the eroded embankment of some few hundred metres, get on the rail track and go through the tunnel. It was either that, or find a way around because there was no way over the sheer rock cliffs. The reasoning behind our decision was that tracks go as straight as possible and that the track was definitely along the same line as the non-existent Wall. About halfway up the slippery slope, which was like clambering over marbles, we heard a long rumbling sound that grew increasingly loud, like the low boom of a didgeridoo.

A train was coming. It popped out the tunnel almost above us like a giant, scaly, black snake. A very long black snake! I couldn't believe it, as the train literally just kept coming for minutes. The snake's twin diesel heads – like a Medusa-headed monster – had disappeared around the long curve of the buttress and still its body came out of the dark rock. I guessed it to be at least three kilometres long.

'Geez, what if we're in there and another one comes through?' I panted, struggling up the slope.

'Could be a problem,' replied David, a little anxious.

'Let's just do it,' I said.

'I agree, I don't feel like backtracking a second time today,' said David, stating the obvious.

Getting onto the bridge was a dangerous undertaking on its own. There was an almost sheer rock wall of I guessed 10 metres. It was the cemented foundation under the tracks before they entered the tunnel. Although only 10 metres, a fall would send us tumbling down the steep stony incline we had just ascended. There were plenty of hollows between the chiselled rocks where I could get decent four-finger grips, but it was free climbing and David wasn't keen.

I am a fairly competent climber so went first. Leaving my pack at the base, I looped the rope over one shoulder and climbed slowly as David fed out the slack. Once up, I tied the rope around a pole and hauled first my pack and then David's up to the tracks. Looping the rope through the railings to create a friction brake, I gave David the thumbs-up. He had his harness on and was tied in. He began climbing. As I top-belayed him I couldn't believe his improvement. He was calm and confident. Ensuring he had a hand and foot placement at all times, he scaled the rough wall like a pro. The rope probably just gave him confidence. I joked with him about the day on the climb out from the Yellow River when he would freeze up on the rock and start shaking. My buddy had come into his own in the mountains. He was strong and confident and it was great to see.

Peering into the blackness I expected to see 'light at the end of the tunnel' – there was nothing.

'I thought tunnels went straight,' I said.

'Hey, this is China, China, anything can happen,' he joked.

With our head lamps on, we entered the monster's lair. The sleepers were spaced 'Chinese' – they were too close together for us to step on each one at our natural pace, but not close enough to reach each second one. So it was either a fast-paced small Chinese step, or we had to stretch really hard. We couldn't run, it was just way too dangerous as everything was foreshortened by our head lamps.

Every 200 metres or so there was an alcove, an indentation cut away into the rock, sometimes plastered with a domed roof but often just a carved-away catacomb-like hollow. They were eerie. They made me think of graves waiting for the living. Strange, what unfamiliar dark places do to you when your eyes can't make sense for the mind. After chatting about it in the echoing blackness, we drew the conclusion that they were cut out as shelters for the railway maintenance crews who would be stuck in there when a train rumbled by.

Garmin had lost his satellite connections so I had no idea how far or fast we were travelling. Looking at the time, we had been in the snake hole for more than an hour. I'm not claustrophobic, but then again, I'd never before been in a situation like this. I wasn't feeling great though; the air was warm and my breathing wasn't relaxed.

'How you doing?' I nonchalantly asked David.

'It's really musty in here,' he replied.

I was getting worried. This was taking a long time and we still couldn't see any light. I had to stop and change batteries. With David's light on me, I opened the zip-lock bag and took out the three new ones.

It started slowly, the gentlest vibration. I almost wasn't sure if I'd heard anything. I stopped moving and tilted my head to listen. Then it echoed down the tunnel like a didgeridoo coming from far across the desert.

'Train,' we both said together.

I had no idea which side it was coming from because I couldn't see a light and the noise was all-enveloping.

'Let me finish,' I said, as David checked left and right, leaving me in the darkness to fumble with my head lamp.

'Sorry, hurry up.'

No kidding! I switched on the lamp.

'Go, go, find a hollow,' I urged, as the earth shook around us.

Then the light came towards us. Like a meteor pin-prick in space, heading for Earth, it got rapidly brighter and the noise got louder, a lot louder.

Standing in an alcove, I yelled to David to block his ears. We had switched off our head lamps because we didn't want to be seen. When we had entered the tunnel there was a skull-and-crossbones sign with some Chinese writing under it. We didn't need to understand the words, we knew what they meant: 'Dangerous; keep out; go away!' The noise was deafening as the train drew closer. The whole tunnel lit up in an eerie white light that seemed to ricochet off the dark walls. They looked as though they were covered with black high-gloss paint.

I had a flashback of being in the tunnel of doom at the fairground as a kid, only now we were the poor dead standing in the nooks and crannies. Then the monster snake ate the light as it passed, so close that the hot air tugged at my clothes. There had been no wind in the tunnel, until then. The train sucked air as it rumbled along, which stirred up coal dust. I could taste the coal. I pulled my bandana over my face like a bank robber and groped for David to show him but he was already ahead of me. We stood in the inky blackness, eyes closed tight, hands over ears and breathing as lightly as possible. It seemed like 10 minutes but was probably closer to five when the last lumbering coal truck sucked past us with a *whoosh*.

Then the wind! The long metal serpent had created a massive vacuum behind it. As we moved back onto the tracks, we hit a serious headwind. The train had come from the opposite direction as the previous one, although there was only a single track. We later saw double tracks outside the tunnels, which allowed for the trains to pass. The trains going east carried coal, those returning west were empty. We walked into the wind, which was so strong we had to lean into it for at least the following few minutes. Then we saw the faint glimmer of light at the end of the tunnel. We exited 20 minutes later.

Breathing fresh air again felt really good. Including waiting for the train to pass, we had been in the black hole for around two hours. David and I looked like coal miners. Our faces were black with soot. Garmin linked the points and filled the gap and we saw we had covered only six kilometres in that time. That was about one kilometre every 20 minutes.

'That was pathetic,' I said. 'We've only done 30 kays in total and it's already 3 o'clock.'

As we moved out into the sunlight David's fear of heights returned. I must say, I wasn't exactly ecstatic at what I saw in front of us either. The tracks went straight from the tunnel onto a seriously high bridge about a kilometre long before it vanished into another tunnel on the far side. There was no way up the sheer rock wall. We had no choice but to move forward.

On the left of the line was a narrow platform of maybe 60 centimetres wide, clearly built for maintenance workers who had no problem with working high up. The walkway was constructed of a series of concrete slabs laid into a metal frame running parallel with the tracks. I hesitate to use the word 'concrete' because it was so brittle in places that pieces had broken off, showing only flimsy wire reinforcing.

Peering through the gaps I could see a thin ribbon of a river with wide sand banks about 100 metres below. Keeping our feet as close to the metal frame as possible, we moved slowly across the bridge. Walking on the concrete sleepers was even more hazardous as there were big gaps between them.

'Geez, I hope a train doesn't come now,' said David.

'Thank god there's no wind,' I said. 'Imagine being here with that howling wind we had yesterday.'

From the bridge David pointed out a watchtower on the mountain directly ahead of us. The 'Wall' here was just a series of watchtowers as no construction could follow these cliffs. The mountain itself was more than enough of a defensive barrier. Even building the stone watchtowers on the high points must have been a serious accomplishment.

No train and 20 minutes later we walked past the second skull-and-cross-bones sign and into another gaping hole. As we entered I heard another train, this time from behind us somewhere in the long tunnel we had come from. We hid in the very first alcove, which was no more than 100 metres in and followed the same procedure as earlier. The good news was that, on entering, we could immediately see daylight at the other end. So, while we still had to endure the 'long train wait' as we had in the previous tunnel, this time it was not a complete unknown and was not nearly so frightening.

The line exited the tunnel onto a wider area of pastureland flanked by mountains. We picked up a pre-plotted GPS position 4.2 kilometres to the right and climbed down the embankment onto a 'dinosaur' track heading in the general direction of the team. Dinosaur was the name David had given the three-wheeler mechanised workhorses of rural China. They come in different sizes and are mostly blue. With one wheel in front and scooter-like handle bars, there is space for two people next to each other. The cab is usually covered and occasionally has doors. Behind the cab is the bakkie that is supported on two wheels. They really look prehistoric, like something from *The Flintstones*, hence the name.

Walking the last few kilometres to camp, we reminisced over the previous two days and spoke about friendship. David likened it to an onion, him being a chef and all. He spoke of how we think we know someone, but often it is based on the first few encounters in the beginning of the relationship. I suggested that it is often through sharing hardships with someone that real friendship is born.

'It's like peeling off the layers of the onion, one at a time, until you reach that soft pit in the centre,' David said. 'It's only then, when you can be open enough to share your deepest feelings with a friend, that you really connect.'

It was nearly dark when we saw the lights of our camp. We walked in silence for the last kilometre but I felt more connected to my companion than I believe we had ever been in our friendship spanning some 20 years. By that point in our journey we had covered more than 3,000 kilometres together, with something like another 1,000 still to go. This had indeed become a multifaceted journey: it would continue to bring me new lessons that would determine the path of my life for years to come.

29

Hitting Back

BECAUSE OF THE DAILY AND VARIED PRESSURES on all of us, there were still occasional quarrels and arguments between team members, but we were closer than ever as a group. We had all, in our own ways, learned to accept each other's differences and value each person's unique input. Like the parts in a reconditioned engine, we had to be readjusted, the individual pistons properly synchronised and the whole tuned to finally function smoothly. Over the past few months, we had learned to focus on a common goal: to finish this enormous undertaking. Although, almost unbelievably, two-thirds of the run had already been conquered, there was still a substantial way to go. I realised how important it was for each team member to be acknowledged, not only for their valuable contribution, but also for their individuality.

We humans are social creatures by nature. We desire acceptance and to be valued by others for who we really are. This is the basis of any successful relationship, and the start of real friendships. I say *real* because, too often, we associate with people for the wrong reasons: 'What can I get from this person?' or 'What's in it for me?' instead of relating to and complementing their unique gifts and talents.

I am not suggesting we should only be giving to a friendship, what I am saying is that what we give and get back should be based on lasting values and principles rather than the feeding of status and egos. For me, that's the difference between real friends and those who are acquaintances. There should be no jealousy or secret agendas in friendship; only positive reinforcement and support. The giving and the taking should be in easy harmony. When they are not, or you feel uneasy about them, you will know they are not in harmony.

'Love is a doing word,' said the Lebanese poet and philosopher Kahlil Gibran. I believe it is and try to live my life by it – in my friendships, my relationship and especially with my son. I thought a lot about friendship in the days that followed. I remembered the exercises I give the kids who come on camps in the bush with me and the scouts that often camp at Appleton on weekends.

Every day they would have to spend an hour alone in nature and complete certain tasks. On their first day out, they would begin and end the hour with a three-minute exercise.

First, sitting comfortably, they would close their eyes for one minute and concentrate on everything they could feel – like their feet on the sand, the wind on their face and so on. Then, secondly, opening their eyes, they'd concentrate on everything they could see – without looking around, just on what was in front of them. Finally, again closing their eyes, they'd focus on all they could hear. This simple exercise was something I had learned many years earlier and still practise today. It enhances my senses, calms my mind and provides me with as great an appreciation of nature as of myself. It is a simple start to meditation. After this, they were asked to think of their friendships.

They had to draw a circle on a sheet of paper. Inside the circle they had to write the names of their closest friends. On the reverse side of the page they had to write 'asset/liability'. Underneath, they had to write if they thought they were an asset or liability to their friends, and vice versa. The exercise causes you to put a value to each friendship, positive or negative. It makes you think about what your friends bring to the relationship, or indeed what the relationship is worth in terms of time and energy invested. It also makes you question whether you add value to their lives or what your contribution should be in the lives of those close to you.

I do this exercise myself, usually once a year or so. It helps me focus on friends who are assets in my life and then plan to spend more quality time with them. If, on the other hand, I feel I am not bringing value to a relation-ship, then I need to question why I am in it. I have friends who I see only every few months or so, but they bring value to my life and, sometimes, huge value to others.

One such person is my friend Jaco van Deventer. Jaco works for Cape Nature and is based in the small town of Porterville in the Western Cape. To me he is a real example of a 'salt of the Earth' person. Ever since I met him many years ago he has been a 'giver', not just to me, with his knowledge, but to nature itself. Jaco goes way beyond the call of duty. He often pays for his own fuel, which he can ill-afford to do, to go and rescue an animal in distress sometimes many hours' drive away. He has unselfishly saved many leopards from almost certain death and, when necessary, it is he who must end a distressed animal's life.

He educates children as well as farmers in proper conservation practices. His modest home is also a temporary sanctuary to many injured animals that he has rehabilitated and released back into the wild. It is people like Jaco who, in their quiet and modest way, lead by example. He is but one example of people I know who simply go about their daily lives being an asset to the world around them.

Another is Robbie Oosterbaan, whom I have known since I was 10 years old, yet has remained constant in his values all the years. Although we see each other only a few times a year, we know that we can call each other anytime, and he will be there at a drop of a hat.

And Belinda Guillot, who believed in me when I had nothing financially, yet understood my spirit. We connected in the higher places – and now we still connect – feet placed firmly on the ground but still soaring in the heavens. A friend forever.

And also Peter Fox, who did my marriage ceremony and became my friend – because he availed himself to walk a path of common ground with me and taught me the value of 'differences'.

We have much to learn from people like them and would do well by showing them our appreciation.

Sometimes we stay in relationships, whether a friendship or a partnership, for the wrong reasons. The sadness is that when we do, we shut out other opportunities and possibilities to learn and grow. We are creatures of habit, and changing things scares us and is often painful. It is important to distinguish the good habits from the bad and to act when we realise the bad ones are preventing us from reaching our fuller potential. It has been a lesson I have had to learn over and over before I finally got it!

Sometimes we are meant to walk a path with someone for many years, even most of our lives. At other times we, or they, feel they need to move in a different direction. It is the wise soul who understands this, and the brave one who accepts it and acts accordingly.

When my ex-wife Louise decided our relationship wasn't working and asked me for a divorce, it felt as though my guts had been ripped out. I struggled to breathe, got hot flushes and wanted to die. I lost my dignity and, for months, begged her to change her mind.

'I can change,' I would say.

I believed that as long as it was all my fault, then I could change and save the relationship. But it is seldom only one person's fault that a relationship starts to unravel, and our marriage was not to be saved.

Again, in hindsight, I learned a valuable lesson. A year later I had moved beyond that relationship. I needed to be on my own. I needed to start to love myself again for who I was, not for what others thought of me. I needed to be able to feel centred and whole before I could truly give worthwhile company back to someone else. Unintentionally, Louise had given me a valuable lesson and a gift for which I am thankful. As a result of our letting go and our openness over the years, we remain special friends today.

Friends should be able to communicate with honesty. They often show us things we are too afraid to see and give us a different, more wholesome perspective on life. In many respects, nature has been my most constant friend. Nature always puts things in perspective for me and helps me re-evaluate what's really important. Its ancient language speaks with an unfailing honesty that transcends words.

Having lived in my home at Appleton Camp on Signal Hill in Cape Town for more than 20 years now, I have been exceptionally privileged to live in a natural paradise, partially sheltered from the madness of the city below. Living in the only house on the hill, within Table Mountain National Park, overlooking ocean and mountain and with the Cape Town city bowl tucked just out of sight below, I am fortunate I have been able to keep my connection with nature almost on a daily basis. I can go down to the ocean, just 10 minutes away, and dive under it or take my surf ski and paddle on top of it. Or I can run from my garden gates along the ridge and up Lion's Head.

Almost daily, I think about endemic plants that only grow only on this one specific piece of rock in the world, and see birds of prey hovering weight-lessly in the updraft blowing up the side of the hill from the ocean. Coming home at night, with the clouds rolling across the road like candyfloss, I have surprised porcupine mothers with their young, owls patiently sitting in the branches of trees waiting for rodents to cross the road, and even caracal startled by the headlights of my car right in my driveway. I can sit on my veranda and watch the sun go down over the ocean, without the sound or sight of another human being. In this way, I am soothed by nature's balm every day.

Often people drive up onto Signal Hill in their cars at night and park at the edge of the road that follows the side of the mountain above the city. They look down at the sprawling apron of lights that covers most of the vista, up to where the rocky contour of the mountains fade into peaceful darkness. They are in awe of the beauty of the city's sparkle, but what I notice is the constant hum of the electricity, the noise of cars and the smell of the fumes that casts a pall over anything natural. Many will not notice the stars above. Or the owl sweeping past silently in another world.

Many people live in a reality completely apart from the natural world. Their reality stops where the darkness starts, them on one side of Signal Hill Road and me on the other. They don't conceive beyond what is in their immediate interest, what serves their comfort or their entertainment. They live in an illusion that was created for safety and perverted by greed.

Through the course of civilisation, nature started off as a danger and a threat that needed to be controlled; as someone once said, to be driven from the door. From there it graduated to being used as a resource, and what was not convenient or useful was killed or laid waste. Eventually, so little was left, and it was so far removed from our everyday lives, it became a curiosity. Now, so little remains of raw nature, bio-geographer David Quammen has likened the natural world to a quilt where all the stitching has come out, the pieces have all become separated and the edges of each piece are now fraying. Continents have themselves been sliced up into numerous small islands of nature, and they are almost all now under threat of survival.

As a species, we have forgotten how we rely on nature for our lives every second of every day: not to mention the air we need to breath. In our compulsive quest for comfort and convenience, we have created a great divide between ourselves in artificial surrounds (homes, clothes, fur coats, heaters, air-conditioners, ice-makers, automatic can openers, robotic vacuum cleaners … the list goes on and on) and the natural world. Mostly we fail to see how each bit of our intricate man-made jigsaw puzzle is destroying our resource base: clean water, forests, grasslands, seas, the atmosphere.

In our minds we own the world like a piece of property, a car or a TV that we can use at our discretion. We are arrogantly oblivious to the fact that we didn't create the world and that we are just another species of animal, subject to the laws of nature, no different to the rat or the grasshopper. We may be a superb predator and possess intelligence and organisation on a level way beyond our relatives, but we can't make water or manufacture our own air without the intricate processes that nature provides – many of which we still do not fully understand.

Many people see nature as existing somehow apart from themselves, maybe above, to be revered or loved. Or maybe below and to be feared, or tamed. Many people – and even whole cultures – see her as something with unlimited resources to be exploited and squandered for our own use alone. Think of photos you may have seen of fishers on a beach somewhere surrounded by the dead bodies of so many fish you cannot count them. Or hunters with big guns and big grins standing behind the piled-up carcasses of antelope. They did not believe that bounty would ever run out, but it has.

Of course we need to exploit the raw materials of nature to make our lives bearable, but that has never meant one party wins and the other loses. The wise watchwords have always been 'sustainable use' and 'limited wastage'. By moving so far away from nature in our modern urban lives, and through the economic system of chasing the highest share price, we have instituted a process of environmental pillage and maximum wastage. How many of us grow any of our own food, recycle all our household waste, make compost from garden and kitchen waste, have planned indigenous water-wise gardens, have timers on our geysers, use solar power for heating water and so on? The way we are living now cannot be sustained.

Sometimes it is confrontation that can lead to enlightenment and growth. Often, through confrontation, we are presented with the opportunity to change. Change allows us to evolve if we embrace it positively. When Sir Edmund Hillary confronted Mount Everest, it changed not only him but also inspired and changed many others. The same can be said about when mankind defied gravity and landed on the moon, or when Roger Bannister broke the four-minute-mile 'barrier'. Things perceived to be impossible force us to challenge our own limitations. They make us question the very nature of these barriers, and to see that maybe there was no real barrier at all but rather a challenge, that a barrier is really just the uncertainty or fear we have of the unknown. For most people that will cause them to see a wall, while a few will see a door that dares them to step through.

Challenging nature in a positive way, such as climbing Everest or crossing a stormy ocean, surfing a giant wave or riding a thermal column of air with a paraglider, feeds a hungry, searching soul. Challenging her in a negative way, overexploiting her resources by destroying forests or polluting the air, causes her to hit back hard at us.

This is as true on a personal level – be it Tenzing Norgay and Hillary daring their skills and their lives on Everest, or David and me on our run across China, or on the level of a whole society. Throughout history there are examples of cultures that overexploited their environmental resources (almost always the trinity of natural vegetation, soil and water). In some cases, including the Mayans in Central America, Anasazi of southern USA and the Zimbabwe stone-building culture of south-central Africa, it has led to the demise of entire civilisations. And now we – all of us alive today – are assisting in the pollution of the land, the seas and the skies as we go about our daily lives. Each one of us is unaware, or only partially aware, of the cumulative effect our individual actions (not to mention the huge industries that cause massive daily environmental harm) have.

But the difference for us, in this modern age of super-information, is that we cannot claim we didn't know. The Mayans depleting their soils with each new patch of forest cut to make a new field, or the Anasazi growing beyond their water supplies, did so in small cocoons of knowledge. But we *do* know about the forests and the fishes we're depleting, as well as the plastics and the poisons we're pouring out to choke nature. We know we are destroying our Earth and yet most of us still cocoon ourselves in our synthetic worlds in the vain hope that the harm done will all somehow go away. But this does not absolve us of our guilt. *Only positive action will.*

I also believe that when we challenge ourselves in the embrace of nature, we show the Earth respect. It brings us closer to her in ways that enhance us beyond words. I believe nature shows us our potential and gives us humility beyond the ego we build based on our material trappings. Nature offers us solutions to every problem; but in order to understand this, we need to regain our perspective as tiny creatures at the mercy of the elements, rather than as masters of the stock-market universe. When we push nature away we enter into a relationship of unknowns and fear, which robs us of our potential for bold action. But miracles abound around us, being discovered every day, if we look.

Yet when we do attempt the impossible – like my friend, Pete van Kets, paddling 500 kilometres across a mighty ocean in a pea-pod boat, with the mountainous waves and howling winds showing him his vulnerability – I believe we realise our truth: that we are not small and alone, but rather huge and connected to all things. That is why, when someone does a great thing, we admire them. It is because they remind us of our own potential. They remind us that we are naturally human, connected and capable of doing amazing things. They remind us also of what we have lost in growing up and being forced into places much smaller than those we dreamed of when we were children, that we have forgotten the innocent belief in personal miracles, and that life can be magic if we choose it to be so – and why should it be otherwise?

I would often think, on the high mountains when we were into the last third of our quest – especially when I was in pain: when I finish this I will have achieved a world first. But what does that mean, really? For me, to achieve something that has never been done before, something that is physically and mentally debilitating, is valuable for personal growth. It endorses my belief that anything is possible. I feel closer to nature, to my Maker, and I draw great comfort from that. At least as important for me is that it serves as an example to others that they are capable of doing something similar themselves. It helps children to believe in their goals when they see a 50-something old bullet like myself living out my wild-child dreams.

I believe that if more people lived out their own dreams, they too would become more deeply connected to nature. And perhaps if enough of us did, through mass action we could collectively apologise to nature and so rekindle the respectful and loving friendship we once had.

30

Not-so-solid Ground

IT WAS ANOTHER −20°C MORNING as I reluctantly pulled on skin after skin of cold-weather clothing, being careful not to touch the wet interior of my tent. I had left my half-full water bladder under the fly-sheet during the night. It was frozen solid and I had to heat water on the gas stove to thaw it out before refilling it with fresh water.

David and I began the long, slow climb back up the mountain to our last way-point of the day before. By the time we reached the Wall we had done an extra 22 kilometres. This was happening almost daily now but we just couldn't move any faster, what with heavy packs as well as rocking winds and the debilitating cold.

Although the extra distance was messing with our heads, we could still get proper nutrition most nights and sleep warmly – if fitfully. Having decent rest and a 'healthy' fat content in our food was now vital to our success. The support vehicles sometimes got within a few kilometres of the Wall, but usually we had to wend our way down pathless slopes and through complex valley systems until we found them. In the morning we'd make our way back up. This became another mind-over-matter battle.

I had lost about 10 kilograms and David even more, although he had started off with more body fat than me. We both craved fat in our diets. Pork lard, while not my all-time favourite, became a necessity. I had eaten dog meat, donkey meat, chicken heads and feet ('walky-talkies'), pig intestines and who knows what else, but the pork fat is what I believe saved us.

Around midday I thought I was having a déjà vu moment. It felt as though I had been there before. Then I realised we were on the area of Wall near William's farm where we had been a year earlier, only this time winter was upon us. The trees a year ago had been lush and green, now they were stark and bare and the ground was covered in snow.

'Maybe we will stay at the farm tonight,' I said to David excitedly.

'It's probably about 20 kays away,' he guessed.

'Let's push, we can do it,' I said.

I was keen on a warm bed and a bit of reminiscing. We discussed it but decided to err on the side of caution. Up here an accident was all too easy if we lost concentration. When we left the Wall at about 16h00 the cold, pale yellow sun was close to the horizon and already throwing long shadows. The support team was six kilometres away and I was extremely cold. I picked up the pace to get warmer, jogging whenever I could.

As I wound my way down a narrow ravine I put my foot on what appeared to be solid ground. The snow had filled a hollow and my leg disappeared almost to the knee. I tumbled forward and a sharp pain caused me to shout out. I lay on my back and bit my lip from the pain. This was an old injury that I thought was long-healed. The pain was horrible and it came from directly below my right knee.

Years earlier I had been called to remove a Cape cobra from someone's garden in Camps Bay not far from where I live (catching poisonous snakes and removing them from suburban gardens and houses has become a bit of a voluntary thing I do). The snake – the second most lethal species in Africa after the black mamba – had taken refuge under a large boulder and as I prodded it with my stick it suddenly came out straight at me and struck at my leg. I jumped back, avoiding the bite but landing with all my weight on my right leg.

Something gave way and my knee complained with a loud snap. What I remember now was that the pain was excruciating. Over the months that followed normal running was fine but occasionally, when running off-road, I would misplace my foot on a loose stone and the lateral movement brought the pain back. I had learned to manage it and knew it would pass within a few minutes of the incident. Usually a lump would develop at the back of my leg in the crease of the joint, but this too would subside after a day or two.

Before setting off for China I had gone to see Dr Willem van der Merwe, a top knee surgeon at the Sports Science Institute in Newlands, Cape Town. He had detected a torn meniscus and shaved it clean during minor surgery. He did, however, notice that I had no cruciate ligament in my right knee! That was the loud snap I had heard all those years earlier when catching the cobra.

'I don't see how you can expect to run the Great Wall of China without a cruciate ligament,' said a concerned Willem. 'But it's too late to put a new one in before you go. You won't heal in time. The best you can do is try to strengthen your stabiliser muscles by doing a lot of training on the Grucox machine.' Willem was not at all confident of my ability to run a marathon a day for one week, let alone month after month.

Subsequently I had done many hours on the Grucox before starting the Great Wall run and hadn't even had a niggle along the Wall, until now.

'Not now, not now,' I said over and over to myself as David knelt next to me, lending his emotional support but not sure what else to do.

'I'll be okay, just give me a few minutes and I'll be okay,' I said, slowly trying to bend my knee.

It was the same old familiar pain caused by lateral movement I had experienced years ago. I just hoped it would subside as quickly as it had in the past. I unzipped my outer legging and peeled it to above my knee, then packed snow behind the joint. After about 10 minutes it was comfortably numb.

'Okay, let's go,' I said, leaning on my trekking pole for added support.

My knee was tender but the pain was bearable and, as it warmed up with motion, seemed to improve. I was lucky, very lucky. I had been warned about it and needed to be more aware in future. It certainly put paid to any further ideas about reaching William's place that day.

That night I used the instant-ice that Medac had given us in South Africa. It's amazing stuff: you break a chemical ball inside a plastic blister pack and it mixes with another chemical causing the pack to freeze for up to 20 minutes. I iced my knee on and off for maybe three hours. I took a K-Flenac anti-inflammatory capsule from our Cipla medical bag before going to sleep. I had a troubled night, plagued by worry, but the next morning felt right as rain.

'Just take it easy,' cautioned David.

'No kidding!' I said, as we retraced our steps up the slope towards the beckoning Wall. Light snow was falling and it danced in little pirouettes in the gullies. Another cold one, I thought.

'Just take it easy, one step at a time. Concentrate. Concentrate,' I sermonised to myself.

The day was long, steep, windy and freezing. On the upside, my knee was feeling fine and finally we would be at William's farmhouse that night. The snow swirled through the broken towers and the wind made ghostly sounds. The place seemed surreal. David and I hardly spoke: we often didn't speak much, but now the wind made communication near impossible. I thought back on the year before. It seemed so far away, like another world. Occasionally I would see a familiar tower or remember a broken parapet.

It was a quiet, contemplative day for me and I missed my son terribly.

After what seemed an interminable time we picked up the way-point for the evening. As I trundled down the familiar footpath to the farmhouse, I recalled the silence I had noticed a year earlier. Again, it was around me, all pervasive. No sign of life. It seemed as though the Earth here was dead.

Walking through the old trellised gate made of woven sticks, I could hear the muffled banter of Lilly and Lunga in the kitchen and Lilly's infectious laugh caused me to smile. Then the aroma of warm food engulfed me and I felt an immediate surge of happiness. Warmth, good food and good company and, later, a warm bed heated by a small fire under the cement slab. All the comforts of home, yet not quite the same.

Lilly had excelled yet again and she provided us with a veritable feast. She had gathered an array of meats and vegetables from the villagers down the valley. Most of the meat was pork, but I'm sure there was donkey and goat in there as well. Hans and Michael brought out the accordion and guitar and entertained us until my eyelids drooped. I went to my room, noticing the red door, with the same lock and its beautifully embroidered tassel, that I had passed through more than a year earlier. I lay in the blackness and remembered the feelings and thoughts I'd had about the Wall, high above and so aloof, back then. It seemed like an eternity had passed since that night, and I was a different person.

We had spent so much time in the alien landscapes of China, just running and thinking each day, it felt like we had entered a parallel universe, as if someone else was continuing our 'normal' lives back home. Just as I had felt in the army, reality seemed to vacillate between two different worlds: the one I was in now, and the one I had lived in at home. It was often hard to remember which one was 'real', and it left me in deep confusion and anxiety, trying to find something tangible to hold on to. In these moments, I would think of Benjamin and touch the little round stone. It reminded me of who I was and connected me, like a safety line, to my life back home.

31

Aliens and Demons

IT WAS STILL DARK WHEN I WOKE DAVID and we left in the early greyness of dawn, our head lamps bobbing eerily between the tree skeletons. Michael and Hans joined us, as we were moving towards a tourist area some 15 kilometres away where a support vehicle could collect them. The day was clear and was likely to provide excellent photographic and filming opportunities. We were about a kilometre from the farmhouse when I realised I had forgotten my GPS solar charger. I told the guys to go on ahead and I would catch up. After collecting the important piece of gear I set off at a fast pace.

When I climbed onto the Wall the sun was just cresting the horizon. Snow powdered the ground and had been blown into piles against one side of the Wall. The sun turned the snow on the parapets to silver and gold. The only sounds were my breathing and the steady *crunch, crunch, crunch* of my shoes as the ice crystals broke under my weight. The rest of the guys were out of sight. It was a gorgeous day and I felt a child-like excitement to be alive. I was having a sensory rush and loving every moment. I noticed the orange and grey lichen growing on the stone. I could even smell the rock; it had a flint-like odour. I licked it and it tasted like flint!

Although I could see no movement, no animal, bird or insect, the landscape itself appeared to be alive. I knew it was because *I* felt so alive, exhilarated, free and at peace. Perhaps it was the sense of relief that my knee was okay, or maybe it was an endorphin release after all the stress of the previous two days. Whatever it was, I just wanted it to persist. But, like many good things, the moment passed. It's as though we need the downs to really appreciate the ups.

A while later I saw the others in the distance, about a kilometre ahead. Even at that distance the sounds of their laughter reached my ears. From a high point I could see the Wall had changed. It looked cleaner, newer somehow. Drawing closer, I realised it was an official tourist section. The Wall had been restored and was pristine. Then I noticed a wrought-iron gate with barbed wire looped around the top. Two security cameras were mounted on a pole facing away from me. The gate and cameras, I realised, were to keep the tourists confined to the designated section and away from the wild side from which I was coming.

David, Michael and Hans were now out of sight; clearly they had climbed over the side and were in a dip somewhere ahead. I had no option but to follow. It was a tricky manoeuvre and required a bit of a balancing act to avoid getting hooked on the wire spikes. Once over I ran at a good pace, being sure not to turn round and face the cameras. I caught up with the other guys, who were lying in a 'camera shadow' waiting for me. It was already close to 10h00 and we hadn't yet seen another person. Up ahead we could see cable cars hanging stationary like Christmas lanterns on an electric cable. Rounding a wide bend we finally caught sight of people. There seemed to be a restaurant of sorts as there were rows of blue umbrellas on a terrace. I was concerned that maybe we would bump into some official. We were wearing branded gear and carried backpacks. We certainly didn't look like tourists and we had no tickets to show if we were stopped.

As we neared the cable-car station and restaurant we passed a few curious onlookers.

'Just smile and say hello,' I advised. 'But keep moving.'

David had his camera around his neck and stopped to take pictures.

Good idea, I thought, let's at least act like tourists. Passing by the tourists, all Chinese, we bid 'Nǐ hǎo' and put on our best tourist smiles. None of us had shaved in over a week and looked more like we were on a serious mission (which we were!) than casual foreign visitors. Moving away up a steep section, there were only one or two adventurous folk ahead of us.

'I think we're out of the woods guys,' said Hans.

It was then that we saw them: three uniformed officials, military-looking with the distinctive red band around their hats, moving slowly towards us.

'Cover your Garmin,' I whispered to David.

Hans and Michael had GPSs in their packs, while David and I had them on our wrists. Because of the North Koreans playing with nuclear bombs some months earlier, no tourist was allowed to carry a GPS. The *China Daily* had made a scene of it on the front page. They had deported some Japanese tourists who were using a GPS to get around Beijing. We had scratched off the Garmin sign and used black koki pens to disguise the housing. Ours looked more like watches and we had switched to time mode.

The officials were about 200 metres away. Hans and Michael set up a pose and David snapped away, trying to be a convincing tourist. My stomach was in a knot. If we were stopped and not allowed to continue, our journey would be broken. I could see another gate on the ridge about a kilometre ahead and guessed that the two poles I could see held more big-brother cameras.

We decided to split up: Michael and I walked about 50 metres ahead while David and Hans pretended to take pictures. As we approached the guards we smiled and greeted 'Nǐ hǎo'. They greeted us back but with not so much as a nod or a smile. They reminded me of KGB agents from some movie, lacking any sort of personality at all. We continued up the incline, not looking back for a few minutes. Curiosity got the better of me and I turned round. They had stopped David and Hans. I knew there was no chance of any discussion because of the language barrier.

'Where is Piou now?' I asked Michael.

'Ach, it will be fine,' came his optimistic reply.

David and Hans had started moving again and we waited for them to catch up. 'Those guys are very suspicious,' said an anxious David. 'We couldn't understand a word, so we just said 'xie, xie' (yes, yes – pronounced 'che, che') and kept moving. Don't look back. Maybe they think we're just going to the end point for pictures,' he said.

The gate was less than 500 metres ahead. No-one turned around. With about 200 metres to go we heard the guards shouting behind us. I turned round and they were gesturing for us to return.

'Let's just get the hell out of here,' said a panting David.

It was steep and we were moving fast. Hans had looked around and said they were following us. We all knew they had no chance of catching us so we bolted for the fence. I went over last and made a point of smiling at the camera as I climbed past. I looked back and could see the guards had given up the climb, but I could hear them protesting loudly in high-pitched wails.

Michael and Hans were supposed to have left us, taking the tourist exit. So much for that now! Our next concern was whether the guards had any way of notifying other authorities further along. We put on a serious pace, running wherever possible. I tried calling Piou but got only his voice mail.

We pushed hard, stopping only for 10 minutes to eat. By 16h00 we had clocked 55 kilometres. The familiar *beep-beep, beep-beep* of the SMS was music to our ears. We found a shepherd's path leading away from the Wall and into the valley below. It was about 10 degrees off our way-point but it made sense to follow it as it would be easy going, as opposed to the thorny and rocky option along our dead reckoning.

It turned out to be the right decision as the path came to a gravel road that took us directly to the spot where our crew had made camp. They had been anxious as Michael and Hans had been 'missing too much long'. The crew had gathered wood and had made a fire. As we sat warming ourselves, we discussed the incident with the guards and the day's other events. Hans was convinced they were soldiers and waxed lyrical about his military training in Austria.

Another day had ended and I was closer to my goal.

'One step at a time,' I said out loud as I zipped my tent closed for the night.

When I woke suddenly at 03h00 I was sweating in my sleeping bag and breathing heavily. I had been having nightmares about being in the army.

'That was 30 years ago,' I cursed, trying to bring myself out of the swirling panicky mess in my head. 'Get a grip on yourself Braam, it's gone, over, ended,' I said quietly in the darkness.

I put on my head lamp and tried reading a bit to get my mind off things. I hadn't had a nightmare like that for years. I thought they had finally disappeared but the ghosts had returned, here, on the Wall, in the cold of China.

In the miserable days of apartheid in South Africa, military service for white males was compulsory. After leaving school we had the choice of going straight to the army or studying first. Either way, you did your time. Back in the 70s you joined for one year and then went back for a three-month camp each year for up to 10 years after that. We were conscripted to the army, navy or air force. Some guys went to the SA Police Services. I was put in the army and joined up for three years.

My aunt, who worked for the opposition party to the ruling National Party, had inside news that the one-year compulsory service was to be increased to two years at the end of 1976. And we would still have to do camps (she was proved right). A three-year contract meant an extra year of service initially, but also better pay, more privileges and no camps afterwards. After three months of basic training most 'troopies' prepared for 'border duty' and spent a fair amount of time 'defending' the South West African (now Namibian) border against '*die rooi gevaar*' (the red, or communist, threat).

Leaving the safe environment of a middle-class English-speaking home and school environment, I was thrown into a mix of people from all walks of life, the majority of them Afrikaners. Some had completed their standard

12 years of schooling, while others had only the most rudimentary education. Some were athletes and some were drop-outs. There were academics and farm boys, power-hungry maniacs and frightened introverts. There were even a few boys who had never before used a flush toilet and were not used to washing very often. But there were common denominators that built the backbone of the army – we were all made to look the same and eventually, almost felt the same. Our shaved heads, brown uniforms, brown socks, brown boots, even brown underwear, began moulding us into the beginnings of a military machine.

First we were taught to hate, then we were taught to kill. Under the pretext that the communist threat was going to take our land, our home, we had to stop it at all costs. And 'it' was generally understood to be black people, whether in South Africa or beyond. The generals were the brains, we were their instruments. We were taught what to think, not how to think. It was not for us to question, it was for us to obey and to do. The years of anger, pain, hatred and death eventually made me feel that everyone was mad. Every one of us was blinded and I felt all alone in a mixed up, crazy world where we had long forgotten our true purpose.

The only consolation I found was being in the bush: ours was often referred to as a bush war, because most of us who were called on to do border duty and cross-border incursions got to spend a lot of time in the wild African bushveld. Being close to the animals, trees, birds and insects kept me alive inside. Being alone in the night, lying under a canopy of billions of stars listening to the cacophony of night noises, the *whoop-whoop-whoop* of hyenas, the yelping of the black-backed jackals and the occasional deep, penetrating cough of a lion kept me mildly sane.

After the army, like so many other young men, I struggled to fit back into society. I never talked about 'the war'. We were told that the brave are silent. I kept everything inside. But the pain and the fear would not go away and they came back to me, again and again, as horrible as ever, in the darkness of the night.

I remember coming home on leave after being in the bush for almost four months. I was sitting looking out the window, as though in a trance, at the beautiful plane tree that grew in our back garden. There was a light drizzle and the tree's massive trunk was wet on one side only, as the rain was driven by the north-west wind. Plane trees have a mottled bark that flakes off in patches. The tree was bare of leaves and I was looking at it as a camouflaged, lifeless thing. As I stared, I got a shock. I felt momentarily like I was two people, almost schizophrenic.

I suddenly thought of the tree I had grown up with. I remembered sitting high in its branches in the cool greenness of spring and watching a Cape turtle dove sitting on her two white eggs. I recalled how often I had sketched it, both with leaves and bare, with charcoal. I remembered giving a drawing to my Granny as a present. Memories of the innocence I had once known came flooding back. I thought of the 'little bush' that had been my playground. It was a small strip of natural veld that formed the buffer between our garden-city suburb of Pinelands and a light industrial area. It was where I first discovered nature existing in a balance. I would turn over rocks and find a small snake curled up near a scorpion. In the comfort of dark silence, a sanctuary was shared. In my war years, I found my sanctuary in the wilds of the African bush.

Yet, as I sat there, I saw the tree as cold and dead. It frightened me because it reminded me of my two selves. My happy, carefree, younger nature-loving self and my confused, angry soldier self. Looking back, it was an amazing insight and was the slow beginning of my road towards recovery.

It wasn't all bad. I learned a lot of good things from the army. I learned to blend in with nature, to track, to observe, to hunt. I learned to work in a team and appreciate differences. I learned that hatred never solves anything but only destroys. And, ironically, because of the nature of a bush war, I learned to think for myself. That led to a yearning to keep learning throughout my life and to only make well-informed decisions. I chose not to follow but rather to lead. I have taken much of what the army taught me and used it positively and practically in my life.

I have taught game rangers tracking techniques, how to read the signs of the bush and walk by the stars at night, and how to use a weapon if necessary. I show people, especially children, what it means to be an African. I am an African. This is my home, my Africa, and I am part of this big land. I feel her earthy caress under my bare feet. I embrace her smells and her tastes and I learn, almost daily, the wonderful and endless lessons she offers. Africa is a tough land for sure, but she is also one of the most varied and giving places, with her incredible diversity.

As I lay in my tent in the blustering wind of the freezing Chinese mountains, I was made doubly aware of how much I missed my home. I realised also that the demons of long ago had simply been sleeping inside me. They hadn't died as I'd thought. I swam in and out of restless sleep until the rude, icy dawn pulled me towards another day of aching feet and high, lonely peaks.

On the Wall that next day the memories of the war stayed with me. I tried singing to get the confounded sticky thoughts out of my head. Fleetwood Mac's '*Don't, stop, thinking about tomorrow. Don't stop, it'll soon be here. It'll be here, better than before ...*' helped for a while but, whenever my mind was empty of conscious thoughts, the demons filled the space. I laughed to myself as I thought of the similarity of the Wall and my thoughts. I had indeed built a wall around myself, thinking I could block out the past. It was suddenly very clear that all I had done was wall in the past inside myself.

This journey along the Great Wall of China was a wonderful metaphor. 'The dragon of my past has been sleeping deeply, but last night the great beast woke up,' I mused. Here I was, running along the spine of 'the Sleeping Dragon'. This great, broken wall was offering me a rare opportunity: to break down my walls and go inside and confront my own dragon, not pretend, as I had done for so long, that it had left me.

I spent the next few days reliving the past, feeling all the old hatred and pain well up inside me, and at night in my tent writing down miserable thoughts and past happenings. The nightmares returned in all their fury in the weeks that followed. They were as real to me as the alien landscape I was battling by day, and they consumed me in much the same way.

I consciously relived them in the day, slowly just accepting, allowing myself the prerogative of occasional tears. And with the tears I learned, high on the cold back of the Sleeping Dragon in China, to forgive myself for the many things I had done wrong. And for things that I thought I had done wrong.

By confronting the pent-up anger I had stored inside I realised I had been blaming myself for the indoctrination forced on an innocent 18-year-old boy. I had carried the guilt of it inside me for the next 30 long years and during all that time it was eating away at my spirit like an invisible worm. It had been difficult to analyse, because the pain and guilt had been intertwined with complicated feelings about my family.

It was a long, lonely week as I slowly exorcised my inner demons. And as I understood it – clearly understood it – I let it all go. I could feel that by forgiving myself I was gaining a level of self-knowledge I had not had before. All the while my inner battle raged, it carried me through another 250 kilometres of tortuous Chinese landscape.

TO THE BO SEA

Quenching the Flames

去渤海—火焰滅了

32

Fire and Ice

AFTER NEARLY THREE MONTHS INTO OUR 'GREAT RUN' – as December approached – the weather was predicted to get even colder. By now we were rounding an arc of mountains north of and around Beijing, still several hundred kilometres short of the Bo Hai, or Sea. William had said we could expect the mercury to drop below −35 °C. Analysing the big map of China with David, we calculated we had about 700 kilometres of the Wall left to follow.

'Probably closer to 850, what with all the doubling back to get to the support crew,' I said.

After a lengthy discussion, we took the decision to forfeit all further rest days and to push right through to the end. Any more delays would severely compromise our chances of completing the journey before winter finally closed the door on us. But equally it was a big risk, because no rest in these conditions could also finish us off!

'One long final slog and maybe we can get home by Christmas,' I said, with a hint of nervous excitement in my voice.

It was the first time I tasted the possibility of victory.

'Be careful,' I warned myself, 'it ain't over till it's over.'

One day at a time. One careless fall, one broken ankle, would end it. Many expeditions have failed because of overconfidence ending in unnecessary accidents in the final push. Still, the excitement was hard to suppress. My son was flying in to join us at the beginning of December. He would travel with the team in one of the vehicles and I would be with him most evenings. I was really looking forward to seeing him. I wanted him to share that much-awaited and so often dreamed about last day, when we'd reach the place where the mythical Dragon drinks from the Bo Sea at Shanhaiguan.

There was still a way to go, with some of the hardest terrain ahead of us. The days were short, the nights long, and the wind extremely cold. Combined with incredibly steep gradients, it all dictated a painstakingly slow pace. In places the steep, narrow steps of the Wall were iced over and sometimes we'd take an hour or even more to inch our way up just 200 metres. Patience was a key factor at this stage of our journey, where one slip would almost certainly end in death.

At one point I rounded a buttress to find the Wall had broken away on one side, with only a narrow row of bricks left perched precariously one on top of the other. A steel ladder of some 30 metres had been built in more recent years and spanned the open gorge between the walls. The gradient was around 70 degrees. The only problem was that the left side, both top and bottom, was no longer cemented in. The lower foot was hanging in space, with a blob of concrete clinging tenaciously to the metal. I tugged on the ladder to test its reliability. It protested squeakily as if it wanted to be pulled free from its top anchor.

'Hey, this isn't good,' said David.

'I'm going to slowly hang on it to see if it will take my weight. Move back a bit,' I said.

I gently began applying my weight to the bottom rung. It groaned at me as though it was alive. It swayed slightly but took my full weight as I hung off the ground.

'Okay, I'm going up,' I said. 'I'm sure as hell not going back down.'

I slowly climbed the broken, rusted ladder, keeping my weight as far to the right as I could.

Each step I took was greeted by a groan. Finally it was David's turn. He didn't accept my offer of the rope and slowly made the ascent unassisted. Again, I was impressed with his new-found courage with heights.

By the end of our first week of 'no rest day' progress we had covered about 320 kilometres, albeit really arduously. After 10 days of travel like this we started really feeling it. The tiredness at the end of each day was shattering. I seriously felt we had made the wrong decision and that we should return to our old regimen of one rest day a week, but said nothing. We both looked and felt like zombies. Our faces were gaunt and our eyes appeared dead and recessed in our heads with hanging bags of skin under them. After two weeks I adapted to the new regime because I started to feel the exhilarating sense of the end being close and somehow got a second wind. I was stronger on the uphills than ever before.

Another big bonus for me was that Benjamin had arrived and that had buoyed my spirits and given me something, and someone else, to connect with. He was enjoying his time with the gang and his happiness was

■ THIS PAGE: The country's culture
fascinated me, particularly the ancient
architecture and the Buddhist monasteries.
When possible on a rest day, I would talk
to children or simply interact with them.
They lightened my spirit and motivated
me to move forward.

■ **ABOVE AND RIGHT:** Rural accommodation on rest day often comprised a stable-type dwelling. Sometimes, I would use the 'bush bath' filled with bottled water.
BELOW: The special moment that touched Michael's heart: a blind boy, intrigued by the sound of his harmonica, reaches out. They held hands and Michael was humbled.

■ **THIS PAGE:** Iconic, well-maintained tourist Wall was such a contrast to the desert Wall, where often we would meet peasant farmers that had chiselled their simple homes into the mud Wall itself.

■ **THIS SPREAD:** The finish! Fourteen pairs of shoes later I reached the sea. The exhilaration was incredibly emotional. Suddenly it was over. Symbolically, we poured the water from the Great White River into the Bo Sea and clasped hands in quiet acknowledgement of the giant we had conquered.

■ **A COLLAGE OF MY LIFE:** It has been immensely enriched by a connection with and deep love for children and nature.

ABOVE AND LEFT: Having fun with kids in Mozambique.

BELOW: My beloved son Benjamin and the sketch I did for him on his birthday at an oasis in the Gobi desert.

ANDRÉ CRONJÉ

■ **CLOCKWISE FROM TOP TO BOTTOM:** A leopard cub at a sanctuary. The snake I caught in the Gobi on my birthday. The man I rescued from a fire on Devil's Peak (unfortunately neither he nor his wife survived). Doing a nature talk for the children at my Beaverlac sanctuary.

HENK KRUGER/CAPE ARGUS

DEON MAARTENS

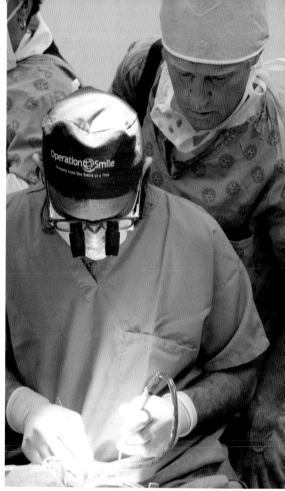

■ **THE REASONS BEHIND MY JOURNEY:**
'To change lives one smile at a time'
and to show people, particularly
children, that ordinary people can
achieve extraordinary things. If you
dream big, plan well and take risks,
nothing is impossible.
ABOVE RIGHT: Watching Dr Anil
Madaree operating on Michella.
BELOW: Before her operation; in
recovery; and six months later.

GEOFF DALGLISH

BENJAMIN MALHERBE

BENJAMIN MALHERBE

OPERATION SMILE

infectious, I think for all of us. He just hated the cold. I had missed him so much. His deep eyes, 'huh huh' laugh, bear hugs and distinct wonderful smell. We didn't need to say much, we just connected and loved. He filled my loneliness and his presence injected me with a renewed energy. I felt invincible.

At the pace we were going, we calculated we had about 10 days left, which would mean finishing around mid-December. I could scarcely believe it and didn't want to entertain thoughts of success quite yet.

Crossing frozen rivers while making our way up to the Wall in the early hours each day seemed easy enough, until one day, close to the end of a hard day, tragedy almost struck – again.

Coming off the Wall with the team just eight kilometres away, we came to a frozen river a little wider than most of the other streams we'd encountered. It was about 40 metres across, with a jumble of ice slabs about 10 centimetres thick that had been shifted and pushed up against one another and were stacked at various angles, all frozen together. It must have been created when the river first started freezing and the slabs formed and broke up as they flowed downstream. There were gaps where I could see the river still flowing underneath.

We tentatively checked the stability of the ice and it bore our weight quite easily. David was not following me directly but was slightly off to my right. I heard a sharp cracking sound, followed by a screeching noise, like someone running their nails down a school chalkboard. It reverberated up the valley in a fading echo. Turning, I saw David slew off a large ice slab, slip through a narrow gap and, in a flash, drop into the icy water beneath. I thought he was gone, but he seemed to hang there, up to his thighs, unable to move. I moved towards him as fast as I could on the slippery, convoluted, solidified river. A whole section of ice was breaking and twisting as though some great beast below was shrugging the frozen stuff off its back. By the time I reached David, he had managed to pull himself to safety.

'There are rocks under us,' he gasped breathlessly, 'and the water's still moving down there.'

I could hear bubbling and cracking and creaking. The ice to our left was still solid and we moved across to it. Reaching land, David stripped off his wet pants and leggings. I gave him my second inner top to dry himself, which he did vigorously.

'Rub hard and fast,' I said as I worked on his other leg, which felt like I was rubbing a block of ice.

'I can't feel anything,' he said, with what seemed to me unnatural calm.

'Just keep rubbing,' I said. 'The circulation will come back.'

This dragon we had taken on might pretend to be sleeping, but every time we thought we had dealt with the worst of it, it would awaken and seemed to have a new weapon in its arsenal to hurl at us.

Fortunately there was no wind and after about 10 minutes or so of massaging and stretching, David started warming up. I gave him my second pair of socks and my loose outer black longs. He used two zip-loc bags, which earlier had kept our food, as socks. With only five kilometres to camp, I knew he would make it.

'If it had been deeper ...' I said, shaking my head.

'Ja, I might not be here now,' said David quietly.

I shuddered to think about it. Had there not been rocks just there and had the water been deeper, he would have slid through the gap and disappeared under the ice and I would not have been able to get to him. 'I'm so sick of this cold,' David said, 'give me the dryness and the heat any day.'

I agreed, but then thought about it for a while. The whole Earth was warming up. 'What is it really going to be like?' I wondered.

In ancient Greece, the name given to the goddess of the Earth was Gaia. For many Greeks, she was the most revered goddess of all. In the 1970s scientists James Lovelock and Lynn Margulis proposed the Gaia theory: it is a view, now widely supported, that sees the Earth as a living organism made up from the totality of all its 'organs', including the oceans, the atmosphere, surface rocks and inner core and including all the individual life forms on it. This field of research is known as earth-system science.

Gaia is seen as an ever-evolving system that strives to regulate the surface conditions of the planet so that they are favourable for life. All life, not just humans. The current environmental crisis facing humanity and many other species is the greatest we have yet experienced. This crisis, as Lovelock puts it in his book *The Vanishing Face of Gaia*, is '*the consequence of putting human rights before human obligations to the Earth and all the other life forms we share it with.*'

My journey across China opened my eyes to the wholesale destruction of our natural resources in our attempt to increase our living standards at the expense of the wellness of the planet. The Earth is currently struggling to support the almost seven billion people that are alive right now. Current best estimates are that we need 1.3 Earths to supply the resources for every person alive today to live at a decent level. By 2050 there are expected to be more than nine billion of us. As they say, do the math.

These are harsh and frightening facts, but I choose to be forewarned so that I may be forearmed: as I mentioned earlier, in the Chinese word for crisis, the *cri* means fear or danger and the *sis* means opportunity.

Having crossed the desert and now, nearing the end of the journey along the Great Wall at the sea at Shanhaiguan, I face choices: do I continue my life as I did before, bumbling along somewhat blindly in a world that I feel is out of control? Or do I strive to lead a different life and to make a difference?

If current global changes means only the fittest will survive, then I would like to think 'fittest' means those people willing and able to live sustainably. I still dare to dream that we can each make a difference and help to reverse the sorry direction in which we are steering our planet. It is similar to my preparation for China: I had the dream and then I diligently set out to get fit so that I could undertake the journey. Although many Earth scientists believe we are only now starting to do 'too little too late', I believe now is the best time ever for us to embrace the view I hold so steadfastly: that 'nothing is impossible' and that 'it is never too late'.

Journeying through China, I saw how the human mind could achieve unimaginable things. Building a wall across some of the most difficult terrain on the planet is surely one of the most manifest examples of the human spirit overcoming appalling adversity. Most of our great achievements begin from single acts of inspiration or leadership, but they are made real through the buy-in of many.

Although China highlighted for me many of the problems facing our planet, it is vitally important that we stop pointing fingers at others and, rather, urgently start implementing best practices at home. Obviously, we should still hold world leaders and governments accountable, but we each need to act locally. My home, South Africa, and indeed Africa as a whole, will not be spared the hard times ahead.

As I neared the end of this journey I looked forward to the start of a new journey: that of being a protector of the natural world that is sacred to me.

33

The Old Dragon Drinks

WE WERE NEARING THE END. We had been going for 25 days without a rest day. My feet were begging me to stop but I was no longer paying them as much attention as I had previously. The understanding that I was going to finish this thing – that I was going to conquer the Sleeping Dragon – was so exhilarating it again showed me the power of the mind.

But why was I feeling so strong when I should have been so broken? Why did I feel I was invincible and could go on forever? It's not that I didn't feel shattered at the end of each day; I did. It was more the promise of victory that drove me. A part of me felt numb to the physical pain because the other part, the elated self, was just that much more powerful. I felt incredibly focused, alive and sensitive to things around me, whereas for much of the run up till now I had been anaesthetised and inward-focused.

Talking with Benjamin in the evenings, I tried to articulate my feelings.

'I know it's not quite over yet, but I'm feeling really alive and I know I'm going to finish it. I know this has changed my life positively,' I said with much emotion and conviction.

'I'm proud of you, Dad,' he said, 'and I'm happy for you. I know you will do it, I never thought you wouldn't,' he said calmly.

Then, 'Are you going to draw again when you get home?' he asked, 'because you know you should. You aren't fulfilling that gift.'

Benjamin was right, I hadn't sketched or painted for years. I had been living in my logical, left-brain world for too long. Again, he amazed me with his sensitive insight.

'I will,' I said, knowing it was an important aspect of myself – to create.

I had always thought best when I let my mind wander. It was as though I wasn't the one controlling it; as though my intuition guided me. It was great, in those last few days, to connect with my son again.

I had dreamed so long for this journey to end and it was coming agonisingly close now. The Wall here was magnificent – bricks packed high, fitting together like a colossal Lego structure. I marvelled at the architecture and thought of those people so long ago that had shaped this incredible beast. The Great Wall is known as the Wall of Tears because of all the people who died building it. It is the longest graveyard in the world. Running high on the buckling Wall the next day, I thought I could smell the sea. I knew it was still some three days' trek away, but the wind was coming out of the east and there was definitely a saltiness in the air.

'So near yet still so far,' I said to David.

Jiayuguan and the desert seemed a lifetime away; another world in another time. I was nearing the greatest physical achievement of my life and I began thinking about how I would feel afterwards. I felt strange and, in a melancholic way, an impending emptiness. I wondered where my life would lead when I returned home. I had planned so much in my head during the journey, but now also felt I should resign myself to providence. I thought of my cabin at Beaverlac and yearned to sit in the stillness of the warm summer evenings and just be. I promised myself there and then to do exactly that, to gather my thoughts and my strength.

The world beyond incessant running was becoming real again. Practical issues outside of the expedition had to be considered. We had called our travel agent, only to find that all flights home before Christmas were fully booked. We were wait-listed and my friend Amanda bugged the travel agent every day. Neither David nor I wanted to sit around in the cold of Beijing for Christmas. Benjamin would be going home as his flight had already been booked. We could just hope for the best. Then there were press releases to prepare and setting times to meet our sponsors and the media once we got home. But that all still seemed weird and far away.

So 25 days without a break became 26. And then 27. Then 28. An then – I cannot say suddenly, because there was nothing sudden about it, but until it happened it could not be dwelt upon – it was my last day on the Great Wall of China. What was unknown to me, however, what I still could not grasp at that triumphant point in my Great Run quest, was how the day following the last day on the run would become the first day of my new life. It was −10 °C but the day was crisp and clear with a bright blue sky. It started with the same monotonous routine as before, but I was excited and stepped into the cold day with an energy that was unstoppable. I wanted to climb the last peak and see the ocean. I wanted to be there, at the end where the tired dragon dips its head into the Bo Sea to quench the flames of its temper, and to savour that salty air and sea water. Suddenly I was also tired of it all and just wanted it to be over, to finish, *klaar*!

The last stretch of Wall was broken and loose underfoot and the going was slow. We arrived at the base of a small, rocky outcrop. We unpacked the two flags we had held above our heads at the start at Jiayuguan almost four months earlier. Each of us tied a flag to one of our trekking poles and placed them symbolically in our packs, and so we commenced our final ascent. The wind was blowing briskly and the flags fluttered out and shone brightly in the sunlight. Cresting the peak I saw the Wall ahead of me wind down steeply and there, across a long flat plain about eight kilometres away, was Shanhaiguan and the silver shimmering sea.

'Yes!' I whispered, 'at last'.

The last few kilometres were flat and easy and we moved briskly. Running up the steps to Old Dragon's Head where the Wall ends in the sea, I could hardly speak.

I was holding back tears when I said to David, 'We've done it.'

We ran the last stretch to where the Wall enclosed us and turned around – there was nowhere further to go. David and I embraced. We left the Wall and walked across the small stretch of sand to the sea, the magical-sounding Bo Hai. Carefully walking out across the rocks, I took the bottle of water we had filled to signify the start of our journey at the Great White River in Jiayuguan from David's pack. We both poured the water into the ocean. I looked up at the last rounded piece of Wall, the Old Dragon's Head itself. Then I looked across to where the sea lapped the Old Dragon as it drank from the ocean, just as we had been told it did.

We congratulated one another and, with tears in our eyes, beckoned for the team to join us. Champagne was shared amidst tears and laughter. Benjamin and I hugged each other. There were no words necessary.

People who were there when the Great War ended on the 11th day of the 11th month in 1918, said that when the mighty artillery barrage that had hammered France just about every day for five years suddenly stopped, the silence sounded like God speaking. I cannot say I heard God speaking to me there at Old Dragon's Head – even though I had had more than my fair share of spiritual insights during the Great Run. But just as suddenly, it seemed, there was a great stillness surrounding me. I could finally put my feet up, both literally and metaphorically. My long march was over. It was 15 December 2006.

34

Into the Future,
One Smile at a Time

IN LATE 2007 I UNDERWENT EXTENSIVE KNEE SURGERY. I had started experiencing frequent sharp pain in my right knee whenever I ran on loose, undulating surfaces. Again I sought the expertise of Dr Willem van der Merwe. An MRI scan showed the hole where my anterior cruciate ligament – one of four bands that holds the knee together and one that is often injured by long-distance running – was supposed to have been.

'We need to put in a new ligament to stabilise the knee,' said Willem.

But when he opened the knee he found the situation was much worse than that: all the running in China had worn down the cartilage (the hard white surface that acts as an anchor for ligaments and protects bone ends where they meet in joints) to such an extent there was bone-on-bone contact in my knee.

Because cartilage has no blood supply, it is almost impossible to repair through surgery. Over the past few years, however, surgical procedures have been explored that help to postpone the need for joint replacement. Also, bioengineering techniques are being developed in attempts to grow artificial cartilage.

After my operation, though, the prognosis was not good.

'I don't think you will be able to run again,' Willem said grimly. 'Certainly not a marathon. We can work on stabilising the knee by using the Grucox machine, but I doubt the cartilage will regenerate sufficiently.'

I informed Willem that David and I planned to run the entire coastline of South Africa the next year, using the same running pattern we'd used in China of running a marathon a day six days a week followed by a rest day. Willem thought I was being unrealistic and felt that it would not be possible.

I chose to believe otherwise and began extensive training on my old friend the Grucox machine. I went ahead and planned as though nothing was amiss. Our main sponsor in China, Cipla, teamed up with Spar and the Cipla/Spar Miles for Smiles Coastal Challenge was born. Toyota became another vital part of the team, supplying four support vehicles, and Engen the fuel.

On 8 October 2008, David and I completed a second world first by running the shape of a 'smile' around the coastline of South Africa, covering 3,278 kilometres from Oranjemund on the Atlantic Ocean to Ponta do Ouro on the Indian Ocean in Mozambique.

A little way before the 2,000-kilometre mark I received a call from Willem.

'I'm hosting a symposium at the Sports Science Institute for about 50 knee surgeons. They are here from a number of different countries and I wondered if I could use you as a case study?' he asked.

After all Willem had done for me, I was only too happy to help. He showed the photos and video of my operation to the other doctors and asked them for their prognoses.

All of them – including a world-famous surgeon from Vale in the USA, Dr Steadman – believed I was a sad case. Dr Steadman said that if I was comfortable in my day-to-day activities, that was fine, but he said I would never run again. The day he said that, I was crossing the 2,000-kilometre mark near the small holiday town of Wilderness.

Willem believes, as I do, that the mind can heal the body. I believe that ordinary people achieve extraordinary things when they free up their minds of perceived limitations.

Round Table took on the project nationally and helped raise about R2.5-million for Operation Smile Southern Africa. More than 500 children from rural communities in southern Africa born with facial deformaties would get to smile for the first time in their lives. The expedition along the coast of South Africa was so much more personal than my experience in China had been. For the first time I got to meet the children face to face and watch their miraculous transformations, both on the outside and in their hearts.

After running through East London, we took three days off and drove to the hospital in Mount Frere where I interacted with many of the children we were funding. It was heart-wrenching when, after the screening process, many of the children, some of them terribly disfigured, had to be turned away because there just wasn't enough money.

One young girl particularly stood out for me. She was sitting away from the other children, who were all accompanied by their mothers. She had been brought there all the way from Cradock, some 250 kilometres away, by her father. They were sitting alone on the lawn when I approached them. Her small frame was slumped, with her shoulders drawn forwards from years of trying to hide her face. At nine years old, Michella was too embarrassed to speak, covered her mouth with her hands and battled to make eye contact. I spent hours with her during the screening process, just telling her stories and holding her thin little hand during various examinations. She told me that she had few friends, along with other stories of disappointment and loneliness.

But when the roster went up on the final day with the names of those selected, Michella's wasn't there. On enquiring, I was told that she was indeed scheduled for an operation but her file was missing. I panicked, searching for her file, but it couldn't be found. Then she and her dad vanished. I ran through the long corridors of the hospital, frantically searching for them. Finally, after a few hours, I found her sitting on a hospital bed with her file in her lap. It was a tough close call because the roster was chock-a-block and there was no more space. After operating non-stop for 16 hours that day, way past midnight, Dr Anil Madaree agreed to fit Michella in.

I carried her light little body into theatre and promised to stay with her until she woke up. She was shaking she was so frightened. As her pretty dark brown eyes closed into a dreamless sleep, I promised her she would be beautiful when she woke up.

Four hours later Michella looked at her new face in a small mirror I held for her, and big glistening tears rolled down her cheeks.

A few months later Michella wrote me a letter saying how her life had changed, that she had come such a long way from hiding away and always fearing other people's stares. She had found so much new confidence in herself and was discovering talents and passions she had not previously been able to explore. She now wanted to 'pay it forward' by becoming a doctor so that she could fix other children's faces one day. She had been given the gift of a new life and all she wanted to do now was to selflessly inspire and help others.

The simple gift of a smile lights not only children's faces but also their hearts, and they emerge from the transformation for the first time able to feel and live their God-given innocence. They are special children, after what they have been through, and many of them end up as leaders in their communities. They don't take things like education and freedom for granted, like so many of us do. As Operation Smile says, 'We change lives one smile at a time.' In turn these children change the world, one smile at a time. I guess we could all do so much better with our lives if we just had a little more of their humility and gratitude.

While running the shape of a smile around the beautiful coastline of my country two years after my Great Wall epic, I spoke to many fishermen. The story was always the same: 'There are fewer fish, things are changing,' they would say.

One day, on Transkei's Wild Coast, an old woman said to me: 'The sea is not giving so much any more. There is not enough to feed our children.'

I realised then that, while changing human lives one smile at a time, if we did not address the seriousness of our planet's plight, there would be very little for the children to smile about as they grew to adulthood. Indeed, there will be very little for any of us to smile about.

We are stealing our children's future in the name of materialism and greed. We think a solution will be found by someone else, and so do little ourselves to bring about the very necessary changes: fewer children, less material wealth and wastage and, most important, more respect for all life in the knowledge that all living things are connected and totally interdependent.

My journey across China and my journey around South Africa are both now things of my past, but they have opened the door to the greatest and toughest journey ever – fighting for the health of our only home, planet Earth.

Epilogue

WRITING THIS BOOK has given me another channel to share what I have learned over a long, eventful journey to greater wisdom. I wanted to impress on people that each one of us has the power to effect a positive impact and make our mark on the world. Every action, every choice we make, no matter how small, leaves a permanent change in the state of the universe.

I don't think many of us take the time to consider the magnitude of the responsibility that accompanies free will and the intellect to understand the consequences of our actions – an attribute unique to our species. I feel that not many of us want to. But considering the planetary degradation that has followed our explosive population growth, we no longer have the bliss of living in ignorance of our powers.

We have all the information in the world at our fingertips. So why don't we start using it to our advantage and find out about what we are actually doing? I call it 'being conscious'. Is it not time for our species to evolve to this level?

You don't have to spend hours each day researching consumable goods you would like to have. Use common sense. Be aware that every business in the world is trying to maximise its profits. So everyone tries to produce items as cheaply as possible. Remember that the people producing your goods are victims of the same disconnection as you are. They also don't really know where the raw materials for their products come from, or what happens when their items start breaking down in a landfill. Most of them don't really care as long as their customers are happy and willing to pay the price they are asking. Everything else becomes a cost factor in the manufacturing chain.

Whether it is people, animals, soil, space, air or water, it is used to make something that can be sold. Looking after any of those inputs and using them sustainably, without causing them to be harmed or destroyed, is usually expensive. That's why organic produce, Fair Trade coffee, hybrid cars and free-range eggs are more expensive than the exploitative equivalent of the same product.

And that usually is the crux of the matter. But in all fairness, if you were able to purchase this book, you are probably in the top 1 per cent of the richest people on the planet with an income of more than US$1 a day and daily access to food and clean drinking water. We are the people who are causing the greatest proportion of environmental destruction and damage to the atmosphere. And we *do* have the knowledge, resources and, hopefully, the enlightenment to make better choices.

Globalisation and world trade have given us the power to affect things far beyond our perceived immediate reach. And because of this temporal and geographical disconnection, our negative influences become easy for us to ignore. It is up to you: whether you want to be aware of this and take back your power to shape the world in a positive way every day; or whether you live in denial while your choices create suffering and destruction on the other side of the planet.

I ask that you become more conscious and aware at all levels of your decision making. Decide what legacy you want to leave behind, long term and at the end of every day. I list just three things you can do that are easy to implement and are extremely impactful. I hope you find some ideas that you will use in your life and share with others to pay it forward and hasten our evolution. We don't have much time.

Food: 'You are What You Eat'

How you feed yourself and your family is one of the most significant areas in which you can make a difference. The power of the consumer over business is enormous and often underestimated. It is not the big corporations, economy and government who make the decisions about what we consume; it's the masses of customers who decide: if there is no demand for something, it won't be produced.

Reduce your intake of meat and dairy products. It really is a win-win change. Firstly, it is exceptionally beneficial to your health. In developed countries, we eat far more meat than our bodies are designed to handle, causing diseases such as heart disease, cancers and diabetes. Furthermore, meat produced in modern agri-businesses is usually laden with antibiotics, contributing to the emergence of 'super-bugs' with resistance to most available antibiotics. Increasingly, hospitals are battling with incurable infections, due to the presence of antibiotics in our food and environment.

We are also the only animals on the planet that continue consuming milk after childhood. Milk is designed to facilitate rapid growth in the infant. Continued consumption into adulthood causes obesity and ubiquitous food sensitivities and digestive as well as respiratory tract problems.

Secondly, greenhouse gas emissions caused by livestock farming surpass the amount released by all the world's vehicles. The amount of faeces produced by livestock is also becoming an increasingly serious problem, running off into waterways and the ocean, creating dead zones devoid of all life, which is in turn affecting fish stocks.

You can still enjoy animal products, however, especially if you are blessed to live in a country with a bounty of wild herbivores. Buy venison. It's healthier because it has not been fed antibiotics and it's cruelty-free. So are free-range eggs. At the same time, you are supporting the preservation of the original diverse wilderness, rather than the veld being converted to monoculture grass lands, feeding only sheep and cattle.

Buy Less – Live More

Don't get trapped in the world of consumption and materialism. Stop defining yourself by what you have and start finding out who you are. True happiness *does* come from the inside.

Grow your own vegetables and at the same time teach your children to reconnect with and appreciate nature. Raise them with values and spend time on them, not money. In this way you also reduce the copious flow of plastic packaging from the supermarket to your trash bin. Use organic pesticides and natural remedies instead of the poisons sprayed on your food in conventional agriculture, which in turn will benefit your health.

Reuse and recreate. Don't be wasteful. That includes your car and electricity. Recycle your trash.

Have a Clean Conscience

Buy cosmetics and personal care products that are natural and not tested on animals. Conventional products all too often contain irritants and carcinogenic substances that are absorbed through your skin every day and also eventually land up in the environment, adding to the toxic burden. Animal testing is unnecessary except when employed for medical research. It is often conducted with unacceptable cruelty and under completely inhumane husbandry conditions and is simply unjustifiable.

The same applies to the production of leather goods.

I trust that in sharing my journey, I have left you with something that has empowered you to make a positive difference, which in turn, enriches your life and the lives around you. We are on this journey together.

Further Reading

Ayres, Ed (2000) *God's Last Offer* London/New York: Four Walls Eight Windows

Diamond, Jared (2006) *Collapse* London: Penguin Books

Dodds, Walter K. (2008) *Humanity's Footprint* New York: Columbia University Press

Freston, Kathy (2009) *Quantum Wellness* New York: Weinstein Books (for women)

Giradet, Herbert (ed.) (2007) *Surviving the Century* London: Earthscan

Hartmann, Thom (1999) *The Last Hours of Ancient Sunlight* New York: Harmony Books

Lovelock, James (2009) *The Vanishing Face of Gaia* New York: Basic Books

Lynas, Mark (2008) *Six Degrees* Washington: National Geographic Society

Quinn, Daniel (1995) *Ishmael* New York: Bantam Books

Suzuki, David (2007) *The Sacred Balance* Vancouver: Greystone Books

Ward, Peter D. (2008) *Under a Green Sky* New York: HarperCollins

Zipplies, Robert (ed.) (2008) *Bending the Curve* Johannesburg: Wild Dog Press

www.earthlings.com

www.coolearth.org

www.foei.org (Friends of the Earth)

www.nature.org (The Nature Conservancy)

www.ewt.org.za

www.peta.org

SUNBIRD PUBLISHERS

Sunbird Publishers (Pty) ltd
The illustrated imprint of Jonathan Ball Publishers
P O Box 6836, Roggebaai, 8012, Cape Town,
South Africa

www.sunbirdpublishers.co.za

Registration number: 1984/003543/07

First edition in 2010
Second impression in 2010

Second edition in 2011
Reprinted in 2011, 2013, 2014, 2016

EDITOR David Bristow
DESIGNER Pete Bosman
PROOFREADER Kathleen Sutton
REPRODUCTION BY Resolution Colour Pty Ltd
PRINTED AND BOUND BY
Paarl Media Paarl

ISBN 978-1-920289-43-0

Photographic credits:
Henk Kruger/*Cape Argus*; Deon Maartens for his
Beaverlac material; André Cronjé, film maker
and journalist; Benjamin Malherbe; Cindy
Robkin for her Mozambique material
and Operation Smile. Credits for
these contributions accompany
the relevant image.

The last hill before
the Bo Hai.